Mariachi Music in America

Mariachi Music in America

∞

EXPERIENCING MUSIC, EXPRESSING CULTURE

∞

DANIEL SHEEHY

New York   Oxford
Oxford University Press
2006

Oxford University Press, Inc., publishes works that further Oxford
University's objective of excellence in research, scholarship, and education.

Oxford   New York
Auckland   Cape Town   Dar es Salaam   Hong Kong   Karachi
Kuala Lumpur   Madrid   Melbourne   Mexico City   Nairobi
New Delhi   Shanghai   Taipei   Toronto
With offices in
Argentina   Austria   Brazil   Chile   Czech Republic   France   Greece
Guatemala   Hungary   Italy   Japan   Poland   Portugal   Singapore
South Korea   Switzerland   Thailand   Turkey   Ukraine   Vietnam

Published by Oxford University Press, Inc.
198 Madison Avenue, New York, New York 10016
www.oup.com

Oxford is a registered trademark of Oxford University Press

Library of Congress Cataloging-in-Publication Data
Sheehy, Daniel Edward.
   Mariachi music in America : experiencing music, expressing culture / Daniel
Sheehy.
      p. cm. — (Global music series)
   Includes bibliographical references (p.) and index.
   Contents: An introduction to mariachi culture — The modern mariachi sound —
The social life of mariachi music — Mariachi economy — Viva el mariachi!
   ISBN-13: 978-0-19-514145-0 — IBSN-13: 978-0-19-514146-7 (pbk.)

   1. Mariachi—History and criticism. 2. Mariachi—Social aspects. I. Title. II. Series.

ML3485.S54 2005
781.64'089'6872073—dc22   2004065663

Printing number: 9 8 7 6 5 4

Printed in the United States of America
on acid-free paper

GLOBAL MUSIC SERIES

General Editors: Bonnie C. Wade and Patricia Shehan Campbell

Music in East Africa, Gregory Barz
Music in Central Java, Benjamin Brinner
Teaching Music Globally, Patricia Shehan Campbell
Carnival Music in Trinidad, Shannon Dudley
Music in Bali, Lisa Gold
Music in Ireland, Dorothea E. Hast and Stanley Scott
Music in China, Frederick Lau
Music in Egypt, Scott Marcus
Music in Brazil, John Patrick Murphy
Music in America, Adelaida Reyes
Music in Bulgaria, Timothy Rice
Music in North India, George E. Ruckert
Mariachi Music in America, Daniel Sheehy
Music in West Africa, Ruth M. Stone
Music in South India, T. Viswanathan and Matthew Harp Allen
Music in Japan, Bonnie C. Wade
Thinking Musically, Bonnie C. Wade

Contents

Foreword

In the past three decades interest in music around the world has surged, as evidenced in the proliferation of courses at the college level, the burgeoning "world music" market in the recording business, and the extent to which musical performance is evoked as a lure in the international tourist industry. This heightened interest has encouraged an explosion in ethnomusicological research and publication, including the production of reference works and textbooks. The original model for the "world music" course—if this is Tuesday, this must be Japan—has grown old, as has the format of textbooks for it, either a series of articles in single multiauthored volumes that subscribe to the idea of "a survey" and have created a canon of cultures for study, or single-authored studies purporting to cover world musics or ethnomusicology. The time has come for a change.

This Global Music Series offers a new paradigm. Teachers can now design their own courses; choosing from a set of case study volumes, they can decide which and how many musics they will cover. The series also does something else; rather than uniformly taking a large region and giving superficial examples from several different countries within it, in some case studies authors have focused on a specific culture or a few countries within a larger region. Its length and approach permits each volume greater depth than the usual survey. Themes significant in each volume guide the choice of music that is discussed. The contemporary musical situation is the point of departure in all the volumes, with historical information and traditions covered as they elucidate the present. In addition, a set of unifying topics such as gender, globalization, and authenticity occur throughout the series. These are addressed in the framing volume, *Thinking Musically*, which sets the stage for the case studies by introducing ways to think about how people make music meaningful and useful in their lives and presenting basic musical concepts as they are practiced in musical systems around the world. A second framing volume, *Teaching Music Globally*, guides teachers in the use of *Thinking Musically* and the case studies.

The series subtitle, "Experiencing Music, Expressing Culture," also puts in the forefront the people who make music or in some other way experience it and also through it express shared culture. This resonance with global history studies, with their focus on processes and themes that permit cross-study, occasions the title of this Global Music Series.

Bonnie C. Wade
Patricia Shehan Campbell
General Editors

Preface

I had three purposes in mind when I wrote this book. One was to provide a resource for the tens of thousands of young people seeking to play and to learn about mariachi music. Another was to create a textbook for the rapidly expanding universe of educators responsible for teaching classes in mariachi music to students ranging from university students to middle school beginning musicians. The third purpose was to share some of the beauty, excitement, challenge, and inspiration that mariachi musical culture has to offer with the broadest possible audience, particularly those who know little or nothing about this world of music and experience. For college-level teachers using *Mariachi Music in America* as part of the Global Music Series in their classes, I hope for this volume to engage students in the notion of music being much more than mere "humanly organized sound" by understanding how mariachi music is a window into a world of meaning, an integral part of a subculture of people linked by a common culture, a common passion, and a common profession.

The overarching theme of this volume is to locate meaning in mariachi music in the relationships of its sounds to evolving and multivalent social and cultural constructs, to economic valuation, and to individual expression. In short, *people* give music meaning, or as Bonnie Wade and Patricia Campbell expressed it in their foreword, "people make music meaningful and useful in their lives." The "music" part of mariachi music is embedded in living culture that evolves over time and place, and meaning in the performance and appreciation of the music is most fully found by considering it in the ever-changing contexts of cultural history, social setting and purpose, and the economic forces that govern its circulation. The organization of this volume neatly follows these categories of consideration. Given the range of the intended readership, the language aims to be "reader friendly" while at the same time inviting the reader to look "out of the music box" to the broader swath of history, culture, society, and economy—the world that mariachi music exists in—to find the music's fullest meaning. Calling mariachi a "world" points directly to another important dimension at the heart of this book. It is a world populated by people who produce it and consume it. For professional mariachi musicians at the core of that world, it is a way of life. For many Mexicans and Mexican Americans, it is an indispensable part of many of the most important occasions life has to offer, and in the United States, it is an important symbol that expresses their unique identity in a multicultural society. For others, it may be an occasional form of diversion. Being a "world" implies that there is some common ground of understanding about what the meaning of mariachi music is. At the same time, deriving meaning is a very personal act, shaped by an individual's collective experiences and personal tastes, and the most vivid expressions of meaning usually come from individuals who make up the mariachi world. With this in mind, I felt it important to include the voices of people who make up this world, drawn from many extensive interviews.

The book opens by considering mariachi music "close up" in the introductory and "The Modern Mariachi Sound" chapters, showing how its palette of sounds gives it color, how its collection of musical structures give it shape, how its repertoire of genres implies meaning and affect, and how its set of stylistic parameters distinguishes it from every other music in the world. Looking at these factors across history, I chart how they took shape over the past 150 years and project how they might move into the future. Considering the music's roots and ongoing close connections to the Mexican culture from which it sprang makes it clear that there is broader cultural valuing at work beyond the mere sounds. Stepping back yet further to take in the social settings in which it is performed, in the chapter "The Social Life of Mariachi Music" we see patterns of how, when, and where it is performed, by whom, for whom, and for what social occasions, telling us about the function of the music and what social expectations shape its performance and appreciation. Viewing it exclusively along the plane of its economic value in the chapter "Mariachi Economy: *Al Talón, Chambas, Plantas,* Shows, and *la Mariachada*," I explore how mariachi music is treated as a commodity, a standardized product to be bought and sold, and how understanding something about the economic life that surrounds it yields yet another store of attitudes and expectations that have direct bearing on the sound and public acceptance of the music. And finally, tuning in to the voices of individuals who break with those cultural meanings and social conventions, in the chapter "¡Viva el Mariachi! Tacos with Ketchup or Salsa?

The Challenge of Change" we discover how mariachi music can be a means of *changing* culture and society as well as reflecting them. Considering all these dimensions helps us better understand how mariachi music today is a product of yesterday's evolution, one aspect of a larger cultural hologram, an act that reflects and builds society and a vehicle for action to change the culture and society in which it is embedded.

Like mariachi music in this final chapter, this book is intended to both mirror and change our cultural landscape. It intends to increase the written store of understanding about mariachi music and, in doing so, empower more people to hear, see, and experience the "message" of the music and the cultural world of which it is a part. I believe that the positive, life-enhancing values that mariachi music embodies are strengthened by its being better understood in the fullest of ways: in its sound, its cultural meaning, and its social uses. Greater understanding allows people who are committed to mariachi music as an integral part of their lives to more effectively shape it to best suit their aesthetic, cultural, and social needs and aspirations. For those for whom mariachi music is a tangential, infrequent, or previously unknown part of their life, I hope the book offers a fresh view of an inviting, engaging world within the world around us, both the music itself and people whom it reflects.

ACKNOWLEDGMENTS

This book was by no means the product of lone inquiry and solitudinous creation. In the United States and beyond, mariachi music is a bona fide movement, driven by thousands of passionate, committed practitioners and aficionados. Many of them shared in the development of this work. Nati Cano, a skilled and strong-willed lifetime mariachi musician with a grand vision for the future of his music, was a constant source of information, inspiration, and encouragement. My long-time *hermanos* in mariachi performance and scholarship Mark Fogelquist, Jonathan Clark, and Russell Rodriguez, all of whom have a greater grasp of the details of mariachi history and key personalities than I, kept me on the straight and narrow in my factual details. Musicians (in alphabetical order) Randy and Steve Carrillo, Francisco "El Capiro de Jalisco" Castro, Mario Castro, Héctor Gama, Rebecca Gonzales, Luis González, Frank Grijalva, Margarito "Santa Claus" Gutiérrez, José Hernández, Pepe Martínez, Carmencristina Moreno, Juan and Belle Ortiz, Leonor Xóchitl Pérez, Cindy Reifler, Laura Sobrino, and dozens of other mariachi *compañeros, compañeras,* and aficionados contributed their thoughts, words, and music, inspiring me more than I could ever express in words. And to the late Don Jesús Sánchez, my first mariachi teacher, I owe an abiding sense of the personal dignity, respect for tradition, and humor that imbues the mariachi world. For his contributions to the vitality of mariachi music, his positive vision of the value of mariachi music to his community, and his limitless hospitality to me during my many visits to the ¡Viva el Mariachi! Festival, *ofrezco mi infinito agradecimiento* to Hugo Morales, farmworker, Harvard-educated lawyer, community activist, and founder and executive director of Radio Bilingüe in Fresno, California. Ethnomusicologist Carolina Santamaría contributed to the transcription of interviews, ideas about music and identity, and other helpful advice. My friend and Global Music Series coeditor Bonnie Wade, aided and abetted by Patricia Campbell, offered direction, moral support, and exquisitely tailored prodding to finish this publication, causing me to frequently recall words drummed into me long ago by my dissertation advisor, Dr. Robert Stevenson: "perfection is a dream; completion is a reality."

CD Track List

1. Rubén Fuentes and Silvestre Vargas, "El son de la negra." Mariachi Los Amigos. Peer International Corp. (BMI) obo PHAM.
2. Quirino Mendoza y Cortes, "Jesusita en Chihuahua." Mariachi Los Amigos. Peer International Corp. (BMI) obo PHAM.
3. José Alfredo Jiménez, "El rey." Mariachi Los Amigos, live performance in a small apartment in Manassas, Virginia. BMG Songs, a division of BMG Music Pub., N.A., Inc., obo BMG Music Publishing S.A. de C.V.
4. "Arenita de Oro." Cuarteto Coculense. From *Mexico's Pioneer Mariachis, Vol. 4. Cuarteto Coculense: The Very First Mariachi Recordings 1908–1909.* 1998. Arhoolie Folklyric CD 7036. 1998. Available from www.arhoolie.com.
5. "El toro." Mariachi Coculense de Cirilo Marmolejo. From *Mexico's Pioneer Mariachis, Vol. 1. Mariachi Coculense "Rodríguez" de Cirilo Marmolejo, 1926–1936.* Arhoolie Folklyric CD 7011. 1993. Available from www.arhoolie.com.
6. "La negra." Mariachi Tapatío. From *Mexico's Pioneer Mariachis, Vol. 2. Mariachi Tapatío de José Marmolejo.* Arhoolie Folklyric CD 7012. 1994. Available from www.arhoolie.com.
7. "El son de la negra," *vihuela* rhythm, excerpt. Russell Rodríguez. 2001. Peer International Corp. (BMI) obo PHAM.
8. "El son de la negra," *guitarrón* rhythm, excerpt. Russell Rodríguez. 2001. Peer International Corp. (BMI) obo PHAM.
9. "El son de la negra," *vihuela and guitarrón* rhythm, excerpt. Russell Rodríguez. 2001. Peer International Corp. (BMI) obo PHAM.
10. P.D. "El perro." Mariachi "El Capiro de Jalisco," courtesy of the National Council for the Traditional Arts and Francisco Castro. November, 1990.
11. "Cielito lindo." Mariachi Los Amigos. 2001.
12. Silvano R. Ramos, "Allá en el rancho grande." Mariachi Los Amigos. 2004. Edward B. Marks Music Company (BMI).

13. José Alfredo Jiménez, "Si nos dejan," excerpt demonstrating *vihuela* and *guitarrón* (*armonía*) rhythm. Mariachi Los Amigos, 2003.
14. José Alfredo Jiménez, "Si nos dejan." Mariachi Los Amigos. 2003. BMG Songs, a division of BMG Music Pub., N.A., Inc., obo BMG Music Publishing S.A. de C.V.
15. José Alfredo Jiménez, "Serenata huasteca," excerpt demonstrating *vihuela* and *guitarrón* (*armonía*) rhythm. Mariachi Los Amigos, 2003. Peer International Corp. (BMI) obo PHAM.
16. José Alfredo Jiménez, "Serenata huasteca." Mariachi Los Amigos, 2003. Peer International Corp. (BMI) obo PHAM.
17. Luis Cisneros Alveart, "Gema." Mariachi Los Camperos de Nati Cano. From *¡Viva el Mariachi! Nati Cano's Mariachi Los Camperos*, Smithsonian Folkways Recordings SF 40459. Available at www.folkways.si.edu. Peer International Corp. (BMI) obo PHAM.
18. José Hernández, "La malagradecida," from *Sentimiento ranchero*. Mariachi Sol de México. Courtesy of José Hernández and Serenata Records. 2004. Available from www.mariachi-sol.com.
19. Pepe Martínez, "Tema Mujer 2000," from *La nueva imagen del milenio*. Mariachi Mujer 2000. Courtesy of Marisa Orduño, director/founder. Orduño Productions, and Mariachi Mujer 2000. 2002. Available at www.mariachimujer2000.com; e-mail, mujer2k_director@yahoo.zcom.
20. Common fast duple-meter *canción ranchera* ending. Mariachi Los Amigos. 2003.
21. Common slow duple-meter *canción ranchera* ending. Mariachi Los Amigos. 2003.
22. Common triple-meter *canción ranchera* ending. Mariachi Los Amigos. 2003.
23. Common *bolero* ending. Mariachi Los Amigos. 2004.
24. Common *son* ending, version 1. Mariachi Los Amigos. 2003.
25. Common *son* ending, version 2. Mariachi Los Amigos. 2003.
26. Jesús Guzmán, arranger, "Jarocho II," from *¡Llegaron Los Camperos! Concert Favorites of Nati Cano's Mariachi Los Camperos*. Smithsonian Folkways Recordings SF 40517. 2005. Available from www.folkways.si.edu.

CHAPTER 1

An Introduction to Mariachi Culture

The *guitarrón* player was lost and running late. The two violinists and trumpeter were already tuned up, and our *vihuela* player was fine tuning his strings. We were lined up just inside the door of the modest country club party room, along with several dozen family members and friends of José, who were gathered to celebrate his sixtieth birthday. José and his wife, Frances, were from San Antonio, Texas, and Frances had wanted to mark the occasion with live mariachi music. So she hired our group, Mariachi Los Amigos, for a couple of hours, wanting only five musicians because the room was so small. She did not, however, tell us it was a surprise party until five minutes before José was supposed to arrive. I was on my cell phone, helping Mario, the lost musician, find the parking lot and try to beat José to the party. It was too late, though, and Mario walked in with José right behind him.

We launched into the rousing and festive mariachi melody "El Son de la Negra" (CD track 1) as José's friends laughed at the sight of José and the mariachi musician in his silver-studded black suit walking in together, yelled, "Happy birthday," and gathered around him. Mario hurriedly took his bass out of its case and was playing along with us before we got to the first verse of singing. From the fast, syncopated rhythms of the *son*, we switched to the century-old Mexican polka, "Jesusita en Chihuahua" (CD track 2). Then, as José and his wife walked by us to look at the collage of photos of José's childhood that she had assembled, we started the introduction to the slow, hard-hitting *canción ranchera* (country song) "El Rey The King" (CD track 3). José and Frances stopped in their tracks and turned toward us. They both sang along at the top of their lungs, remembering the words as best they could. "No tengo trono ni reina / ni nadie que me comprenda / pero sigo siendo el rey" (I don't have a throne or a queen / nor anyone who understands

1

me / but I am still the king). They punctuated their singing by imitating the open-arm gestures of the famous *ranchera* singers on Spanish-language television.

The party was off to a good start. Ranging in age from teenagers to retirees, everyone talked, ate, drank, and listened to our music. The Mexicans asked for their favorite songs and sang along. The others, mainly friends from José's office, seemed to enjoy themselves and were taken with the unfamiliar sights and sounds of the mariachi. One man asked if we could play "The Electric Slide," but he didn't seem disappointed when I told him we didn't know it. Then Frances asked if we knew an old Mexican *corrido* (narrative ballad) named "Corrido de Santa Amalia" that she learned when she was a kid. I said no, but we could accompany her if she could sing it. As she sang a line or two, we figured out the right key for her voice, and I took off on the trumpet, playing the piece of melody that she had sung as an introduction, with the other musicians following. Frances sang loudly and well, impressing most of the friends and younger family members who had not seen this side of her. Later, her sister told me that Frances used to sing in public in San Antonio and that she had a fancy *china poblana* dress at home, like those the women *canción ranchera* soloists wear.

After everyone had eaten, several of José's family and friends spoke about him, telling family and workplace stories and joking. When each speaker finished by toasting José, we played a *diana*, a short melody often used as a fanfare to mark a special moment. As the speeches wound down, our two hours ended, and Frances paid us and thanked us for making the party such a special occasion. As we made our way to our cars in the parking lot, the DJ turned up the volume of the oldie-but-goodie tunes that José liked.

MARIACHI MUSIC AND CULTURE

Mariachi music is one of the most extroverted, expressive, exciting forms of Latin American music. In Mexico, with a population of 100 million people, uniformed, professional mariachi musicians sing and play trumpets, violins, and guitars in a myriad of settings and events in every state and every large city. They are hired for serenades, baptisms, birthdays, *quince años* events (fifteenth birthday celebrations called *quinceañeras* in the United States), weddings, Mother's Days, funerals, conventions, store openings, company parties, civic celebrations, and countless other occasions. Politicians hire mariachis for their campaigns. Catholic churches hire them to play the Mass, particularly on Decem-

FIGURE 1.1   *The most common style of* traje de charro *(Mexican cowboy-style suit) that identifies mariachi musicians is black with silver* botonadura *(buttoned ornaments on the pant legs and jacket). Fashioned from lightweight cedarwood, the six-stringed Mexican bass guitar called* guitarrón *is the most distinctive of the mariachi instruments because of its size and its round-shaped spine.* Guitarronero (guitarrón player) Mario Castro prepares in the parking lot outside a social hall in Chantilly, Virginia, where he and Mariachi Los Amigos will play for a wedding reception.   *(Photograph by author, 2004)*

ber 12, the date of the annual tribute to the Virgin of Guadalupe. In restaurants and bars, mariachis sell their musical wares to the clientele for a fixed price per song. In theaters, mariachis accompany singers in concerts and variety shows. And mariachis themselves often get together for a party and play music simply for the pleasure of it.

The mariachi is well known as a symbol of Mexican culture. Plaster of paris statuettes depicting caricatures of mariachis are popular in marketplaces. Mariachi music itself is used to market an unending number of products on the radio and television. When the last old-style Volkswagen Beetle rolled off the assembly line in Puebla, Mexico, in 2003, a July 31 front-page article in the *New York Times* showed a mariachi group serenading its farewell. Mexican films, radio, and television shows take mariachi sounds and images far beyond the borders of Mexico. Since the early twentieth century, government officials have showcased mariachi music to represent a sense of Mexican national and regional culture. Traveling folkloric ballet troupes, such as the Ballet Folklórico de Amalia Hernández, take a mariachi group with them on tour to countries around the world. Mariachis themselves tour to or reside in other countries in North America, Latin America, Europe, East Asia, and beyond.

In the second half of the twentieth century, the United States—and Los Angeles in particular—emerged as a major center of mariachi musical life. Economic opportunity lured many musicians from Mexico. At century's end, the U.S. population of Mexican origin had grown to more than 20 million, one-fifth the size of the population of Mexico, expanding the music's base of support. Social movements, the popular music industry, and marketing ploys to the growing Mexican market have brought mariachi music to the fore of American life. Hundreds of U.S. schools offer mariachi music performance programs, and dozens of annual mariachi festivals occur throughout the Southwest and beyond.

The ¡Viva el Mariachi! Festival in Fresno, California, is one of the most prominent of these festivals, offering a program of instructional workshops leading up to a concert attended by more than 5,000 people. The festival's celebratory, educational, community-building intent provides a window to the central axis of this book: the interconnection of historical, social, economic, and musical dimensions of mariachi musical culture in the United States and Mexico. Three factors especially have maintained a strong baseline of musical continuity across the political border: Massive immigration of Mexicans to the United States, the power of the international recording and media industries, and the fluid travel of mariachi musicians back and forth between the two countries. At the same time, differing historical, social, and economic circumstances on the American side of the border have left their mark on the music and on the way people appreciate it. When Mexican Americans embrace mariachi music as an expression of their special, distinctive identity in a multicultural United States society, for example, they add a dimension of musical meaning and social status different from that in the Mexican context, where everyone is Mexican. As mariachi musicians acclimated to the American cultural environment, changes in performance contexts, repertoire, the social mean-

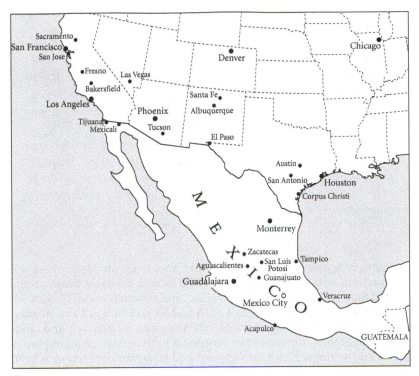

FIGURE 1.2 *Map of Mexico and the Southwest United States, featuring important centers of mariachi music performance.*

ing of the music, ways of learning, and the status of the musician have followed.

Issues for Reflection. Have you ever thought about how music is more than music, that is, more than sounds made for us to listen to? How music is an important part of community life, used to bring people together and make them stronger? How music's space in social life gives it specific, "extra-musical" values and meaning? How musicians themselves are a special group with an identity of their own? How many forms of music are tied to and shaped by economic and business concerns, rather than just musical factors?

ACTIVITY 1.1
Focus on one of your favorite forms of music and address these questions about it. How did you come to know it—television, recordings, the Internet, friends, some other way? How is it part of your social life? Do you think it is important? Do others of your age and background think it is important? Does everyone you know think it is important? Why or why not?

For comparison, think about mariachi music. Given what you know about it, how important is it to you? Is it more important to someone else you know? Why or why not? Try to mentally map out some of the social attachments of music that make it more relevant to certain people.

Pioneering musicians like Natividad Cano, who came from the small town of Ahuisculco, Jalisco, changed the face of mariachi music in the United States. Through skill, innovation, and determination, Cano, with his Mariachi Los Camperos in Los Angeles, and others have planted mariachi music deep within the North American soundscape and landscape and at the same time have molded it to fit in with changing tastes and social settings. Nati Cano knows well how mariachi music is both a product of society and a distinctive culture and is also a force to change the social/cultural landscape. His perspective was key to shaping this book, and his story is an important part of it.

ACTIVITY 1.2
Consider the photo in Figure 1.1 of the mariachi in his typical dress. Do you remember seeing an image of a mariachi before? What was your impression? Was it funny, proud, or exotic, or does it have some other value?

Personal Perspectives of the Author. For reading this book, it is important for you to know how I came to play mariachi music and some of the perspectives I gained from the experience. When I was a college

FIGURE 1.3   *Fresno, California's annual ¡Viva el Mariachi! Festival, launched by the nonprofit Radio Bilingüe in 1982, attracts over 5,000 people each year and offers workshops for hundreds of aspiring mariachi musicians and teachers. On the cover of the 2000 festival program book, artwork by Malaquias Montoya highlights the growing role of women in mariachi music performance.   (Image courtesy of Hugo Morales of Radio Bilingüe. Artwork by permission of Malaquias Montoya)*

undergraduate studying music education, I took a class in the ethnomusicology program, a performance course taught by Jesús Sánchez, an older mariachi musician from the state of Jalisco, in west Mexico. Within a couple of years, I and several other students—Mexican Americans and Anglos—began performing outside the university setting, becoming a working mariachi playing in restaurants, hotels, and many, many other community events and settings. I later founded Mariachi Nuevo Uclatlán as a student group that also went on to perform profession-ally. In 1978, I relocated to Washington, D.C., and founded a new group, Mariachi Los Amigos, that continues to exist at this writing. Over these three decades, I have played mariachi music with Mexicans, non-Mexican Latinos, and non-Latinos, for many mixes of audiences, and for a wide range of occasions, ranging from formal concerts for thou-sands of people, to backyard barbecues, to Latino weddings and other life cycle celebrations. My guess is that I have played mariachi music for well over 3,000 occasions.

My first attraction to the music was the sound of the music itself. Ex-pressive, rhythmic, and with trumpets front and center, it was exciting and engaging. But over time, I became intrigued with other dimensions of the musical experience. For example, oftentimes over the years, some-one from our audience would come up to me and say something such as "You don't look Mexican." This simple comment, repeated hundreds of times, along with many insightful, cross-cultural encounters with Mexican musicians, made me acutely aware of the social dimension of mariachi music. Why, I would ask myself, would audiences not likely tell Chinese cellist Yo-Yo Ma "You don't look German" when he plays the baroque music of Bach, but they would tell me "You don't look Mex-ican" when I played mariachi music? What was different? Why was one music so racialized and the other not?

Being a student of music education at the time, I also began to ques-tion the content of my own public school music education. Why hadn't mariachi music or other "ethnic musics" been included in my music performance and appreciation classes? Were they not "good enough" for the classroom? Who determined what music was included in the curriculum, and why were certain musics chosen over others? With all the passion of a recent mariachi "convert," I became determined to see justice done—that is, to see that mariachi music and other "worthy" cul-turally specific musical traditions be placed on a curricular pedestal alongside the European fine art masters. My naive encounters with the social meanings attached to the music played into my study of ethno-musicology, the scholarly discipline that views music in its cultural con-text and music as culture. They became wedges into the world of mean-ing surrounding mariachi music. Here, in this book, they take shape in the various perspectives from which I have come to understand mari-achi music—historical, social, economic, and musical.

Read what several other people had to say about how mariachi mu-sic fits into their lives and their community:

My father was a harpist with Mariachi Vargas in 1945. My grandfather was a musician, and my great-grandfather as well. . . . I was born a musician. My mother said that I was born singing. . . . And I remember it like a dream, when I was five years old, I already had my little *vihuela* [mariachi guitar] and I sang in fiestas. And professionally, I started when I was eleven years old. I went to school to learn to read music.

—José "Pepe" Martínez, director of the
preeminent Mariachi Vargas de Tecalitlán

[We mariachis] were ignored and insulted. The musicians of the symphony, the philharmonic, saw us as musicians and music that were worthless. . . . It hurt me greatly because I adored and I still adore mariachi music a great deal.

—Natividad "Nati" Cano, director of the Los Angeles–based
Mariachi Los Camperos, speaking of his youth in Guadalajara.

No one is a prophet in their own land. I say that [because when on tour in the United States,] wherever we went, we were like idols, they received us like great artists. . . . It should be here in Mexico where they hold us in high regard for the simple fact that we represent the country. That is not the case.

—Lifelong mariachi musician Margarito Gutiérrez of
Guadalajara comments on the contradiction
between mariachi music's role in Mexico as a
national symbol and the often disparaged
social position of the mariachi musician.

I was working in a bank, as a teller. But I happened to sing a song in a restaurant, and a customer tells me, "Hey, you sing well. Will you sing that song again?" "Will you pay the mariachis?" "I will pay the mariachis." I sang him the song. He reached into his shirt, and the first bill he found, he said, "Here, take it." I look at the bill. It was for 500 pesos. In those days, it was a lot of money. And I took the bill, and I said to the boys [the mariachis], "Listen, it's better here than in the bank." I was making that kind of money [singing], and at the bank I make 600 pesos per month, twenty pesos per day. That's how [my mariachi career] started.

—Heriberto Molina, for thirty years the lead singer with
Mariachi Vargas de Tecalitlán, recalling the economic
incentive that lead him to his career in music.

These heartfelt comments from musicians tell us volumes about important aspects of what we might call "mariachi culture": personal passion for the music itself, music as family tradition, social attitudes that, on the one hand, belittle it as music of an inferior lower class and, on the other, praise it as an honored symbol of cultural identity, as well as economic incentives that encourage its performance. All of these factors play a role in shaping the music as sound. Furthermore, as these factors change over time and across societal differences, so does their impact on the music evolve. For example, while the social elite might continue its centuries-old habit of affirming its worth by belittling people of less affluence—such as mariachi musicians—they nevertheless appropriated mariachi music as a marker of local and national identity and elevated its status and social acceptability. Or, as mariachi music took root in the United States, a new set of social norms meant fresh audience attitudes toward its appreciation and people of culturally different backgrounds bringing

FIGURE 1.4   *In 2001, the three headlining mariachi ensembles at the annual Guadalajara Encuentro de Mariachis were Mariachi Los Camperos, Mariachi América, and Mariachi Vargas, led, respectively, by (left to right) Nati Cano, Jesús Rodríguez de Híjar, and Pepe Martínez.* (Photograph by author, 2001)

their values and worldviews to its appreciation. Those speaking tell us that mariachi music is music and much more—an entire musical and social world rich with personal, cultural, social, and economic values, experiences, and customs that give it meaning.

The Purpose of This Book. This book, then, is about the interconnection of historical, social, economic, and musical dimensions of mariachi musical culture in the United States and Mexico. It is intended to guide you to a deep understanding of this music by exploring its meaning to those who play it and listen to it, as well as its sound. Understanding the evolution of today's mariachi sound helps us understand what is new, what is old, and what people think of as "tradition" (Chapter 2). Appreciating how the music fits into different social situations helps us understand it from the point of view of the culture and society of which it is a part. Chapter 3 will demonstrate to you how the same music can have different meanings for different people, in different social situations, and in different times. Gaining knowledge about how mariachi music is a product that is bought and sold reveals how the forces of commerce can be enormously influential in shaping the musical results (Chapter 4). And finally, having insight into how individuals and communities see the value of mariachi music to their future opens our eyes to how the music is being used as an agent of change to shape society, as well as to be shaped by it (Chapter 5).

CHAPTER 2

The Modern Mariachi Sound

Many people say that mariachi music is contagious, that once you start to play it, it is tough to stop. That's how it was with me. There was something about the sound that appealed to me. Especially sitting in a restaurant like Carnitas Uruapan in Tijuana, with an eight-piece mariachi circled around our table, it was total surround sound, live. Being a trumpet player, I remember being deeply impressed by the energy, the volume, and the rhythmic punch of the two trumpets. The three violins emanated a wall of three-part harmony that I could feel as much as hear. The strumming of the vihuela and the six-stringed guitar was tightly synchronized, crisp, and direct. And the guitarrón—the guitarrón!—*what an amazing instrument! Its sheer quantity of low-end sound filled the room. Add to this a no-holds-barred, expressive singing style, and the result is an unmitigated, direct emotional expression that cannot be ignored. Sitting in the middle of all that, I was transformed. And if the mariachi were to play a fast-driving* son, *someone in the restaurant was sure to let out a loud* grito—*a yell—no more than two seconds into the piece, adding to the excitement.*

—The author

MODERN MARIACHI

The sound of the modern mariachi (*mariachi moderno*) is unmistakable. A rhythmic bedrock of *guitarrón* acoustic bass and the strummed *vihuela* and *guitarra* supports an overlay of hard-hitting, melodious trumpets and a harmony-rich violin section. In a few of the largest groups, the tinkling strings of the large mariachi harp add luxurious color to the overall sound and majesty of its appearance. The musicians play the music their audiences know and love. The *son, canción ranchera, bolero, huapango,* and polka have been mainstays of the mariachi repertoire for over fifty years. Other sounds, such as renditions of nineteenth-century classical music or the syncopated rhythm of the *joropo* (folk music from the plains of Colombia and Venezuela), have added to the variety of mariachi music.

While the mariachi is rooted in rural life of western Mexico in the 1800s and earlier, the modern mariachi sound that we know today emerged during the first half of the twentieth century. In this chapter, you will learn about the origins and emergence of today's typical mariachi sound—the instruments, the poetry set to music, and several mainstays of the mariachi repertoire.

FIGURE 2.1 *Mariachi Cobre, originating in Tucson, Arizona, and now based in Orlando, Florida, performs at the ¡Viva el Mariachi! Festival in Fresno, California. These four instruments—(from left to right)* guitarrón, vihuela, guitarra de golpe, *and six-stringed guitar—comprise the mariachi's instrumental rhythm section, called* armonía. *The rounded-spine* vihuela *is shaped similarly to the* guitarrón *but is much smaller and has five strings. The flat-backed, five-stringed* guitarra de golpe *(struck guitar) was once commonplace to mariachi music but is rarely used in the modern mariachi. The six-stringed guitar most often is paired with the* vihuela. *(Photograph by author, 1998)*

ACTIVITY 2.1

CD track 1, Mariachi Los Amigos playing "El Son de la Negra," is the song the mariachi played at the surprise birthday
party mentioned in Chapter 1. Listen to it several times, until
it is so familiar that you could recognize it if you heard it being
performed somewhere. Then focus on each of the basic ingredients
of the modern mariachi sound in turn: trumpets, violins, vihuela,
guitar, and guitarrón. Can you distinguish each ingredient from
the others?

Before "Mariachi," 1519–1852. The mariachi as we know it today
did not exist until the 1950s. Before 1920, it resembled today's sound
and appearance even less. And in the 1800s, the meaning of the word
"mariachi" was not as clear-cut as it is nowadays. A few historical highlights will give you a sense of the roots that modern mariachi music
draws from.

The Mexican origins of many core elements of mariachi music pre-
date the history of the term "mariachi," instruments among them. In
1519, as the Spanish conquistador Hernán Cortés marched from the Gulf
of Mexico toward Tenochtitlan in what is now Mexico City with the aim
of seizing control of the rulers of the Aztec empire, among his three
hundred men were six musicians. One, a man named Ortiz, was a dance
teacher and player of the viol. Many other musicians, music teachers,
and instrument makers followed. While chordophones (stringed instruments) were nearly nonexistent among Mexico's native peoples, the
Spanish held them in high regard. Various types of guitar, harp, and
violin were introduced to New Spain, as the area approximating much
of today's country of Mexico was called. Instrument making became
widespread, and stringed instruments proliferated. In addition, musical forms, forms of sung poetry, important occasions for music making,
the social value of music, and many other basic building blocks of mariachi music took shape during the three centuries of Spanish colonial
rule (1521–1821).

The Mariachi Emerges. This is deep history. The mariachi's direct
ancestors become better known from the year 1852, the date of the first
known written use of the word "mariachis" in connection with music.
It was in a letter from a Catholic priest named Cosme Santa Anna in

the parish of Rosamorada, in present-day Nayarit state, then under the ecclesiastical governance of the archbishop in Guadalajara (see Figure 1.2), the capital of the state of Jalisco. Addressed to the archbishop, the letter complained of irreverent behavior during public celebrations on Holy Saturday:

> At the end of the Divine Offices in my Parish on Holy Saturday, I find that in the plaza and in front of the church itself there are two *fandangos*, a gaming table, and men who, on foot and on horseback, are yelling furiously as a consequence of the liquor they drink, and all that is a lamentable disturbance: I know that this occurs every year on the most solemn days of the resurrection of the Lord, and we already know how many crimes and excesses are committed in these entertainments, that generally are called in these parts *mariachis*. . . . Then I went to the place of the *fandangos* [dances], I asked for their instruments and they gave them to me, I asked the ones playing cards to stop and they did, and then I also begged them to lift up a poor fellow who was stretched out on the ground drowned in liquor, and they lifted him up. (Jáuregui 1990: 16, translation by author)

The priest appealed to the mayor for help, but instead of putting an end to the festivities, the mayor took up a collection to bring other musicians to replace them. The fresh musicians came and started up another *fandango* that lasted until Monday. Cosme Santa Anna, ridiculed by the civil authorities, returned to the church, rang the bells to assemble his loyal followers, and announced that he was leaving the parish and would help anyone who needed him from the neighboring parish of San Juan Bautista.

The second written mention of the word "mariachi" is in the diary of another priest, Ignacio Aguilar, pertaining to an episode that occurred in the *tierra caliente* "hotlands" area of the state of Guerrero, south of Jalisco. Describing events that occurred on May 3, 1859, the day of the Holy Cross, he wrote that about four thirty in the afternoon, the prefect went on horseback to invite father Aguilar to go with him to a nearby forest area, where the people raised up a beautiful stone cross. "The musics, or as they say around there, *Mariache*, comprised of large harps, violins, and a bass drum, played incessantly. To get to the Holy Cross, there were two parallel lines of stands with refreshments in colored glasses, others with fruits of the region, others with cakes and *empanadas* [meat pie] and sweets (Aguilar n.d.: 125–26, in Jáuregui 1990:18, translation by author).

The number of written occurrences of the word "mariachi" or its variant, "*mariache*," increased over the final decades of the 1800s in descriptions of events in the area around the state of Jalisco. The known uses of the word were not uniform. It seemed to indicate several things in different instances: the occasion at which local musicians performed with dancing (as in Santa Anna's letter); the music itself; the group of musicians playing; or the platform upon which people danced to the accompaniment of the music. To illustrate, in the November 23, 1874, edition of *El Progresista*, a newspaper in Morelia, in the state of Michoacán, a note described a dinner and dance event in the Tierra Caliente region of that state, at which the townspeople of Coalcomán presented their mariachi, "simple and enchanting music, proper to our coastal area [of Michoacán], which when we hear it always brings us sweet memories" (Jáuregui 1990: 20, translation by author). In his 1884 book *Recuerdos de un viaje en América, Europa y Africa*, General Ignacio Martínez recounted a moment during his visit to Guadalajara in 1875 when some young people circulated an invitation for a magnificent serenade in the main town plaza, along with a printed program of the musical selections to be played: "The gathering was large, and as the hour arrived, it turned out that instead of an orchestra, it was that which they call a *mariage*, a kind of street band, comprised of three or four musicians in the distance with out-of-tune instruments. The families present then got the joke and laughed heartily" (16, in Jáuregui 1990: 21, translation by author).

Enrique Barrios de los Ríos, traveling in western Mexico in the late 1800s, described the annual fair and independence celebration in the town of Santiago Ixcuintla (state of Nayarit):

The garden area of the town plaza was decorated and filled with food booths. Between one and another of these shops, there is a *mariache*. This is a platform a foot and a half high, two yards long and one wide, during all night long, and even in the daytime, they dance lively *jarabes* to the sound of the harp, or of violin and *vihuela*, or of violin, snare drum, cymbals, and bass drum, in a wild quartet. Up to four people at a time dance on each platform, and the noisy clatter of the thundering *jarabe* [dance] resounds throughout the plaza and neighboring streets. Songs accompany it at times, and some country people dance it with great adroitness and place upon their head a glass filled with *aguardiente* [alcohol distilled from sugarcane] or an uncapped bottle filled with liquor, and it does not fall off, nor does a single drop spill, in the dance's dizzying turns and other very rapid movements. The *mariache* is surrounded by a crowd happily enter-tained and absorbed in that joyful and noisy dance. (1908:44)

MARIACHI: THE MUSICAL GROUP

In 1905, the four-member mariachi led by Justo Villa from the Jalisco town of Cocula went to Mexico City to perform for President Porfirio Díaz on the occasion of the September Independence Day celebrations. This group, called a *mariachi coculense* (from the town of Cocula), was reportedly the object of much admiration for the liveliness, emotion, and uniqueness of its *sones, corridos,* and songs as well as for the sound of its "violins, *vihuelas,* and *guitarrones*" (Méndez Moreno 132–33, in Jáuregui 1990:30). On October 6, 1907, *El Mundo Ilustrado* reported that to mark the visit of the United States secretary of state Elihu Root with President Díaz, "a *mariachi jalisciense* [from the state of Jalisco] that came from Guadalajara, played *sones* and *jarabes,* and two *charros* [men in Mexican cowboy dress] and two *tapatías* [women from Guadalajara] were dancing to the beat of the harps and the violins" (Jáuregui 1990:30). These citations mark not only the acceptance of the word "mariachi" as referring to the musical group, but the added meaning of mariachi as a symbol of regional Mexican culture, a symbol used by the elite class of that region to represent itself.

The visits of Justo Villa's group to Mexico City had several impor-tant effects. They led to the very first recordings of mariachi music, thus establishing the first audio legacy of the actual mariachi sound. "Be-tween the fall of 1908 and the spring of 1909, all three major American phonograph companies—Columbia, Edison, and Victor—recorded the Cuarteto Coculense [Justo Villa's group] in Mexico City using the 'acoustic' process" (Clark 1998:2). They also presaged a growing mi-gration of mariachi musicians from rural areas to Mexico City and other urban areas. This migration was accelerated by two additional factors: the Mexican Revolution (1910–17) and a massive rural-to-urban popu-lation shift over the twentieth century that made Mexico City, with over 20 million inhabitants, or one-fifth of Mexico's population, one of the largest cities in the world.

The revolution heralded a shift of the position of mariachi and other regional *mestizo* (people who emerged from the mix of cultures) musical traditions in Mexican society, as the new nationalism cele-brated grassroots culture in the writings of Mexican intellectuals and in the symbols exploited by political leaders to represent nationhood. Furthermore, rampant urbanization created a demand for music that

FIGURE 2.2   *The* cuarteto coculense *of Justo Villa was the first mariachi to be recorded.   (Photograph courtesy of Chris Strachwitz and Arhoolie Records)*

appealed to the tastes of the newly arrived people from rural areas, and eventually, as society evolved and as distinctly urban tastes emerged, the sound, repertoire, and role of the mariachi evolved along with it.

ACTIVITY 2.2
CD track 4 is one of the first 1908–1909 sound recordings of mariachi music, "Arenita de Oro / Golden Grain of Sand," performed by the Cuarteto Coculense. Listen to it several times until it becomes familiar. Then, for purposes of comparing it to CD track 1, listen to the mariachi instrumentation. Try to articulate what is similar and what is different. Keep in mind that because of the limitations of the recording technology at the time, the gui-tarrón is barely audible.

The Modern Mariachi Takes Shape.   In 1920, *guitarrón* player and bandleader Cirilo Marmolejo, born in 1890 and raised in the town of Tecolotlán, Jalisco, traveled to Mexico City with his group of five other musicians (Sonnichsen 1993:2). Dr. Luis Rodríguez Sánchez, a lover of *sones* and other music from the Jalisco rural areas, invited the group to the capital and helped them establish themselves there. The musicians named the group Mariachi Coculense, possibly because several of them were from the town of Cocula, Jalisco, or because of the town's notoriety as the home of many of the best mariachi musicians. With the help of Rodríguez, they were able to devote themselves to playing mariachi music professionally in the new setting of Mexico City. This historical moment marked a trend in mariachi history toward groups comprised of full-time professional musicians, and toward the sound of mariachi being that of an urban-based music.

ACTIVITY 2.3
Listen to CD track 5, the recording of the son *"El Toro / The Bull," performed by the Mariachi Coculense de Cirilo Marmolejo in the mid-1920s. How has the sound evolved from CD track 4? Compare it to the sound of CD track 1 and identify what is missing.*

In 1925, the mariachi of Concepción "Concho" Andrade was playing at what would become a legendary cantina (bar), El Tenampa, located adjacent to Plaza Garibaldi in Mexico City. Later, Cirilo Marmolejo and his mariachi joined in, alternating inside El Tenampa with Andrade's group (Rafael 1999:76). Thus began one of the best known Mexican traditions, the daily gathering of hundreds of mariachi musicians around Plaza Garibaldi, serenading willing passersby and looking for clients to hire them for their events. In the 1920s, shortly after the "electric" method of recording music (as opposed to "acoustic," in which sound waves directed into a large horn were converted to grooves on a wax Edison cylinder) came into fashion, Marmolejo's group, under the name Mariachi Coculense "Rodríguez," made the first mariachi recordings in this much-improved technology (Sonnichsen 1993:2). The group also was included in Mexico's first sound film, *Santa*, made in 1931 (Sonnichsen 1993:3). These "firsts" more firmly established mariachi music as a professional form of entertainment in burgeoning Mexico City, and it placed the mariachi more in the arena of the Mexican electronic media, which at the time was on the brink of a major explosion. Over the next three decades, the media—radio and film in particular—would amplify the mariachi's impact throughout Mexico and beyond, and would transform its image and sound into those of the mariachi we know today.

The advent of radio offered unprecedented exposure to these musicians fortunate enough to be invited to fill the airwaves. Within a few years of its launching in 1930, the powerful radio station XEW, "La Voz de América Latina desde México" (The Voice of Latin Amer-

FIGURE 2.3 *Films, radio, and recordings brought the sound of the mariachi to cities in the American Southwest, especially Los Angeles. Mariachi Barranqueño of Los Angeles, comprised of clarinet, trumpet, two violins,* guitarrón, vihuela, *and guitar, poses for this 1941 photo. Third from left is Luis M. Moreno of the well-known Dueto de los Moreno of Los Angeles. His daughter, Carmencristina Moreno, recalls the group performing in nightclubs, public presentations, and private parties. (Used with permission from the archives of El Dueto Los Moreno and Carmencristina Moreno)*

ica from Mexico), began to fill the airwaves throughout Mexico and into Central America. The affordability of radios gave people more access to radio than to record players, and mariachi music reached a much larger audience in the 1930s and 1940s through radio than it had through recordings and live performances. One of the groups heard on XEW as well as on XEB and XEQ was Mariachi Tapatío of José Marmolejo, nephew of Cirilo Marmolejo. After performing with his uncle's group in 1933 at the World's Fair in Chicago, Illinois, he returned to Mexico City and organized his own mariachi (Clark 1993:3). Mariachi Tapatío (*tapatíos* are people from Guadalajara) became a leading group, performing on the radio and in many popular films, beginning in 1937 with *Jalisco Nunca Pierde* (Jalisco Never Loses) and *Las Cuatro Milpas* (The Four Cornfields).

ACTIVITY 2.4
Listen to CD track 6, "La Negra," one of the earliest recorded versions of what is now the most performed of all the sones jaliscienses. Identify the instruments and put into words how its sound reveals the continued evolution of the mariachi toward a professional musical style with more coordinated arrangements and exacting performance.

Instruments of the Modern Mariachi. By the 1950s, the mariachi's instrumentation crystallized into what we expect it to sound like today. Mariachi México de Pepe Villa typified the two-trumpet sound, emulating the grouping of two trumpets, at least three violins (often playing in three-part harmony), *guitarrón, vihuela,* and guitar. While Mariachi México did not use a harp, Mariachi Vargas continued to keep it a part of their group, as they had since the group's origins in 1898.

ACTIVITY 2.5
CD track 2 is Mariachi Los Amigos playing "Jesusita en Chihuahua." Listen carefully. Can you hear all the instruments described above?

FIGURE 2.4   *Mariachi México de Pepe Villa, pictured here at the Xochimilco gardens in Mexico City, was a cornerstone of the modern mariachi sound in the 1950s. The size of the modern mariachi had grown to twelve members, including two trumpets.   (Courtesy of Jonathan Clark, 1950s)*

The instruments and the way they are played are essential to the mariachi sound. The trumpet, violin, and nylon-stringed guitar used in the mariachi are the same versions of the instruments used in orchestras, bands, and guitar classes. The *vihuela* and *guitarrón* are special to the mariachi. They were created in Mexico, and though they were based on earlier instruments brought from Spain, they are unique in origin to western Mexico and are easily recognizable by their shape and sound.

The Vihuela.   The *vihuela* takes its name from a sixteenth-century Spanish variety of guitar that was favored by the educated classes. Over time, "genteel society" came to prefer the six-stringed Spanish guitar, while in western Mexico at least, the Mexican form of the *vihuela* remained in the hands of farmers, ranchers, traders, and the like. As you can see in Figure 2.5, it has a distinctive shape.

The *vihuela* has five nylon strings tuned A-d-g-B-e. Unlike the tuning of the "standard" six-stringed guitar in which the strings are tuned in rising intervals, the *vihuela* tuning goes up, down, and then back up

FIGURE 2.5   *The spined, rounded, convex body of the* vihuela *sets it apart from other kinds of guitar. Its length is similar to that of a six-stringed guitar, though it may not look like it because its body is narrower, as viewed from the front. Its waist is much narrower than the guitar's. Most* vihuelas *are made of a sonorous cedarwood found in many parts of Mexico. It is a lightweight, porous wood that resonates loudly. The top of the soundbox is usually fashioned from a softer wood, such as spruce. Master luthier Roberto Morales, whose instruments are in demand throughout the mariachi world, puts the finishing touches on one of his* vihuelas. *Behind it on the workbench is a* guitarrón *in the making.   (Photograph by author, 1997)*

again (Figure 2.6). Some musicians feel that the purpose of this type of tuning, called reentrant tuning by specialists, is to keep the sound of the *vihuela* in the middle range, so that it will not conflict with the bass line below or the melodies above. This makes sense, since the function of the *vihuela* in the mariachi is to provide a rhythmic pulse and chordal harmonic background to the melody instruments and singers.

FIGURE 2.6   *Vihuela tuning. Notice how the pitches go upward, then downward on the penultimate string, limiting the overall range of the* vihuela *and reinforcing its function of providing mid-range harmonic and rhythmic accompaniment.*

Some of the ways in which the *vihuela* is played are also distinctive. While simple songs and polkas are mainly played with downstrokes of the hand hitting the strings, the fast-driving *son*, the syncopated *huapango*, and certain modern additions to the mariachi repertoire call for

FIGURE 2.7   *The* guitarrón *is made of the same resonant woods as the* vihuela, *and both its volume and its light weight are remarkable. Its volume is increased by the standard technique of plucking two strings at once in a pinching motion. For example, to play an A, the player would pluck the two outside strings (A^1 and A) simultaneously, yielding a bigger sound than if only one string were plucked. In this photo, Rafael Gutiérrez practices* guitarrón *at his home in Guadalajara.   (Photograph by author, 1997)*

more complicated strumming patterns. These patterns, called *mánicos* by the musicians (from *mano* 'hand'), are sequential combinations of downstrokes, upstrokes, stopping the strings with the strumming hand, drawing the fingers more slowly across the strings to produce a flourish, and so forth. Certain *mánicos* go with certain kinds of musical genres, as you will hear below.

The Guitarrón.   The *guitarrón* looks like a big *vihuela*, except that its soundbox is bigger in proportion to its overall length than that of the *vihuela* (Figure 2.5). Also, it has six strings, not five as with the *vihuela* (though *guitarrones* at the turn of the twentieth century and earlier normally may have had five strings).

The *guitarrón* is the bass, playing lower pitches. The tuning is A^1-D-G-c-e-A (Figure 2.8), again, a reentrant tuning, in this case probably designed to keep the pitches of the strings in the lower range. Like most bass instruments in Western European–based musical traditions, it focuses on the main notes of the chordal harmony. The *guitarrón* might play a sequence of pitches with a more melodic character, but they are usually straightforward melodic lines that serve to emphasize the sequence and character of the harmonic and rhythmic framework of the particular piece being played. As in the case of the *vihuela*, certain bass patterns are linked to specific musical genres.

The *guitarrón*, *vihuela*, and guitar together form the "section" of the mariachi called *armonía*, meaning "rhythm section." The musicians think of the *guitarrón*, *vihuela*, and guitar as linked together in a single function, providing the rhythmic and harmonic structure and background for the rest of the music. In this spirit, the three instruments closely interlock, with their rhythms and harmonies complementing each other as a single unit.

FIGURE 2.8   Guitarrón *tuning. The* guitarrón *tuning pattern rises in pitch until it reaches the final string. It then descends, keeping the* guitarrón's *range at the bottom end of the mariachi's sound spectrum.*

ACTIVITY 2.6

CD tracks 7, 8, and 9 demonstrate the sound of the vihuela, *the sound of the* guitarrón, *and how they sound together. The rhythm is that of the* son *"El Son de la Negra" (CD track 1). Focus on the* mánicos *played on the* vihuela *and how they both reinforce the meter and chordal harmonies and add a dimension of musical interest unto themselves. Listen for the greater effect of the* guitarrón *in emphasizing the harmonies by playing simple, rather than complex, lines. Hear and feel how the two instruments interlock and reinforce each other. This is the sign of a good* armonía *section.*

The Harp. The harp is most often seen more than it is heard in the modern mariachi (Figure 2.9). The use of the harp in western Mexico dates to colonial times, when it was a favorite instrument among the Spanish colonials and the *mestizos* who followed them. The folk harp tradition died out in Spain, but it flourished in many parts of Latin America—Mexico, Venezuela, Colombia, Ecuador, Peru, Chile, and Paraguay in particular. Each regional harp tradition is distinguished by differences in the shape and size of the harp, the repertoire, the playing techniques, and other factors. The harp used in the mariachi is similar to that used in the neighboring *tierra caliente* region of the state of Michoacán, in which the harp is a lead instrument. Before the modern mariachi took shape, the harp was often the lead instrument as well in what were called mariachis. Accounts of the mariachi from the late 1800s mention such a harp among the instruments used.

When the modern mariachi emerged in Mexico City, the harp was not among the essential instruments. Mariachi Vargas de Tecalitlán kept it, perhaps because it was a mark of their group's heritage and identity or perhaps because it added visual appeal. Most mariachis, however, found the harp to be easily replaced by the *guitarrón*, since, as mariachi ensembles grew larger, the primary function of the harp was to supply the bass. Another factor weighing against the use of the harp in the modern mariachi was that it is limited to the diatonic scale, that is, it only plays the most basic notes of the scale, not any notes in between. As modern mariachi music saw harmonies get more and more complex, the effectiveness of the harp in supplying a more complex bass line was

FIGURE 2.9   *Five feet in height, a large soundbox with ornamented soundholes in the front, and thirty-six strings covering five octaves mark the Jalisco harp of today. While the harp's role in full mariachi ensembles is today limited to large-scale groups that specialize in concert performances, here the harp is seen performing for clients at the open-air restaurants of the Placita de los Mariachis in Guadalajara.   (Photograph by author, 1987)*

limited. Today, the harp is usually considered to be an *instrumento de lujo* 'a luxury instrument', rather than an essential part of the mariachi makeup. There are exceptions to this around the fringes, occasional throwbacks among some of the older musicians who continue to use the harp. Also, some of the larger contemporary groups are actively experimenting with ways to make the harp once again central to the mariachi musical texture.

Musical Forms. The mariachi plays many kinds of music. Certain musical forms are so characteristic of the mariachi that they help define the essence of its sound. Some of these are the *son, canción ranchera, bolero ranchero, huapango,* and *polca* (polka). These genres are identifiable by the content and mood of the texts (when there is singing), the tempo and rhythmic patterns played by the *armonía,* special instrumental stylistic features, and other factors.

Poetic Forms. Some poetic forms that run deep in history are shared across genres. The Spaniards brought centuries-old traditions of poetic verse forms that were both recited and sung. Two of these, the *copla and seguidilla,* are among the most important in mariachi music.

The Copla. A *copla* 'couplet' was most often a stanza of four eight-syllable lines with the rhyme scheme *abab,* as illustrated by this *copla* from the *son* "El Perro / The Dog" (CD track 10):

(Ay ay ay ay)	
Parece que voy llegando	*It seems like I am arriving*
(Ay ay ay ay)	
Al barrio que yo quería.	*At the neighborhood that I wanted.*
A ver si me muerde el perro	*Let's see if the dog bites me*
Que me mordió el otro día.	*The one that bit me the other day.*

However, there were variations in the number of lines per stanza and in the rhyme scheme. *Coplas* might be freestanding in subject matter—each one a "poem" unto itself—linked to others by a common theme, or arranged in an extensive series to tell a story.

ACTIVITY 2.7

On CD track 10 (Mariachi El Capiro de Jalisco playing "El Perro"), follow the text and listen first for the copla form. Then, listen to how the singing of the simple copla is lengthened through repetition of two-line segments and the interjection of the exclamation "Ay ay ay ay." Through the spinning out of the three coplas and the alternation of sung verse with instrumental renditions of the melody, the musicians create an entire piece of music. Repeating the text also helps the listener understand it.

The Seguidilla.   *Seguidillas* are similar to *coplas* in that they are short and
the second and fourth lines rhyme, but the number of syllables in each
line varies, alternating between seven and five. A well-known example of
the *seguidilla* verse is the following, from the song "Cielito Lindo":

De la sierra morena	*From the dark sierra*
Vienen bajando	*Come down*
Un par de ojitos negros	*A pair of dark eyes*
De contrabando	*Of contraband*

(The word de *and the first syllable of* ojitos *are pronounced together as a
single syllable.)*

Often, when *seguidillas* are set to music, a short repeated phrase is placed
between the uneven seven- and five-syllable lines to adjust to even-
length phrases of the melody. In doing this, the example becomes:

De la sierra morena
Cielito lindo, vienen bajando
Un par de ojitos negros
Cielito lindo, de contrabando

ACTIVITY 2.8
*Pronounce the words of "Cielito Lindo" without the music, count-
ing the syllables (don't count "cielito lindo"), and compare them
to the seguidilla form. Then, listen to Mariachi Los Amigos perform "Cielito Lindo" (CD track 11). Can you follow the text?
As heard here, the seguidilla song form often had a refrain that
followed each of these strophic verses. In this case, it is:*

Ay ay ay ay,	Ay ay ay ay,
canta y no llores,	Sing and don't cry,
porque cantando se alegran,	Because singing,
cielito lindo, los corazones	Cielito lindo, makes hearts rejoice

The Son.   You have already heard several *sones* (CD tracks 1, 4, 5, and
6) and explored the underlying patterns of the *armonía* (CD tracks 7, 8,
and 9). The *son* is perhaps the most important musical genre over the history of the mariachi and has defined the mariachi sound more than any
other form of music. Its importance runs deep into Mexican history.

The first written mention of the *son* as a form of music in Mexico occurred in 1766, when a *son* named "Chuchumbé" arrived at the port of Veracruz with a European fleet that had stopped in Havana long enough to take on passengers and seamen (Ramo de Inquisición 1766: tomo 1052, foja 293). Inquisition documents describe the text and dance movements of the *tonadilla* 'folk melody' practiced by "vulgar people and sailors" that dismayed the religious authorities, who issued an edict prohibiting "lascivious *sones* and obscene *coplas*" (Ramo de Inquisición 1766: tomo 1297, foja 19). A 1779 document describing this *son* indicates that the *son* had caught on in Mexico:

> Let it be known that through denunciations made we know that to us, and extended throughout this city and various other cities and town of the kingdom certain *coplas* are sung that they call the Chuchumbé— beginning "On the corner is standing" which are to a great degree scandalous and obscene, and offensive to chaste ears, and they have been sung, and they sing accompanied with dance no less scandalous, and obscene, accompanied by dishonest demonstrative actions and writhings provocative of lasciviousness, all tending to the ruin and scandal of Christian souls and in injury to the consciences and rules . . . and opposed to the orders of the Holy Office . . . Zacatlán July 8, 1779. (Ramo de la Inquisición: tomo 1297, fojas 19–20)

Forty of these "obscene *coplas*" were preserved. Here are a few of them:

(Original Spanish versions)

On the corner is standing	*En la esquina está parado*
A friar of the Merced	*Un fraile de la Merced*
With his habit raised up	*Con los abitos alzados*
Showing his chuchumbé	*Enceñando el chuchumbé*
This saintly woman	*Esta vieja santularia*
Who comes and goes to Saint Francis	*Que va ibiene a San Franco*
The Father takes, the Father gives	*Toma el Padre, daca el Padre*
And he is the father of her children	*Y es el Padre desus hijos*
I married a soldier	*Me case con un soldado*
They made him squadron corporal	*Lo hicieron cabo de esquadra*
And every night he wants	*Y todas la noches quiere*
To mount the guard	*Su merced montar la guardia*
	(Ramo de Inquisición: tomo 1052,
	fojas 195 and 294)

While certainly not all *sones* were as objectionable to the authorities at the time, these are some of the few early *coplas* from *sones* that happen to have survived. Colonial documents include very little mention of the music created and practiced by New World–born Creoles of Spanish descent, African slaves and their mulatto descendants, and the early *mestizo* people. When vernacular music and musicians are mentioned, it is often because they ran afoul of the stern-eyed authorities of the Spanish Inquisition, who made it their business to watch over the moral behavior of the community. While the spirited, humorous tone of the *son coplas* was muted as they entered the mainstream of musical recordings, many *coplas* with *doble sentido* 'double meaning' like those above have been preserved.

In modern times, *son* texts might draw from centuries-old oral tradition, be invented by rural and amateur musicians, or be written by professional song composers. Older *coplas* may include archaic word usage, poetic imagery that incorporates rural themes, or folk wisdom. An example is the following *copla* from the *son* "El Pasajero":

Yo vide pelear un oso
con una garza morena
que siendo el hombre vicioso
aunque la suya esté buena
no hay bocado más sabroso
como el de la casa ajena

I saw a bear fighting
With a dark heron
For a man who is licentious
Even though what he has is good
There is no morsel more delicious
Than that from another house

The word *vide* is an archaic form of *vi*, "I saw," and the bear and heron imagery reflects rural life. The lines "No hay bocado más sabroso/ como el de la casa ajena" is proverbial wisdom similar to "The grass is greener on the other side of the fence" in English. More contemporary texts often are more self-conscious expressions of pride in a city, state, or region.

Other genres.   Four other essential genres came to the mariachi in the twentieth century: the *canción ranchera, bolero ranchero, huapango,* and polka.

The Canción Ranchera.   The *canción ranchera* rose to popularity with the blossoming of Mexican film and radio beginning in the 1930s. In 1936, the movie *Allá en el Rancho Grande*, a musical melodrama that was original in its stereotypical portrayal of Mexican ranch life, sparked a lucrative period of prosperity and influence in Mexican cinema that lasted into the 1950s. Movie after movie of this, the *epoca de oro* 'golden age' of Mexican film, featured an idealized rural-life setting underscored with *música ranchera* 'country music'. Ironically, this "country music" was mainly an invention of urban songwriters, singers, movie makers, and record producers. Its setting, star-studded casts, and very *mexicano* low-class humor appealed to the Mexican urbanites, some of whom could still relate to their rural roots, or at least appreciated the unbridled, direct sentiment of the *canción ranchera* decrying the pain of unfaithful love, disappointments of life, and simple, country philosophy. The *canción ranchera* is popular to this day.

As a musical term, *canción ranchera* is not very precise. It includes a range of tempos and meters; most often, a *canción ranchera* features one of these variants: a faster, polka tempo or a slower triple- (waltz-like) or duple-meter pattern. Since its core essence is its "country" flavor, it can even be in other rhythms as well. The three main *armonía* rhythmic patterns are shown in Figure 2.10.

ACTIVITY 2.9
To hear the slow canción ranchera *meters, listen to CD track 3, Mariachi Los Amigos playing the* canción ranchera *"El Rey / The King," written by the most prolific of the successful Mexican songwriters, José Alfredo Jiménez, which was sung at the birthday party that opened Chapter 1. This piece incorporates both the slow duple and triple meters. Make a timing chart that shows when each meter is used, then find words to describe the style of singing. It certainly is not introverted.*

CD track 12 gives you the fast ranchera *meter. The tempo of "Allá en el Rancho Grande / There on the Big Ranch" is clearly faster than that of "El Rey." What instruments define the boom-chuck-boom-chuck of the polka rhythmic meter?*

The Bolero Ranchero.   Following the *canción ranchera* in order of significance is the *bolero ranchero*. The *bolero* song form emerged in Cuba

FIGURE 2.10a. Ranchera *fast duple rhythm*

FIGURE 2.10b. Ranchera *triple rhythm.*

FIGURE 2.10c. Ranchera *slow duple rhythm.*

FIGURE 2.10   Armonía *rhythmic patterns for* canciones rancheras. *The tempo marking for each pattern, expressed as a range of beats per minute, gives a sense of the general speed of the rhythms. For example,* ♩ *= 130–150 means a range of between 130 and 150 beats per minute.*

in the 1880s—"Tristezas / Sadnesses" by José "Pepe" Sánchez is credited as the first Cuban *bolero*—spread to Mexico, and several decades later, Mexican songwriters had taken to writing *boleros* of their own. Some consider "Morenita Mía / My Little Dark Woman," written by Armando Villarreal Lozano in 1921, to be the first distinctly Mexican popular *bolero*. The famous Mexican songwriter/pianist Agustín Lara gave the Cuban *bolero* even more of a Mexican flavor in the 1930s and made it a constant, danceable tempo for Mexico's urban nightclub patrons. In 1944, the romantic-style Trío Los Panchos squared off the *bolero*'s Cuban-derived syncopated rhythm, setting the basic pulse of today's *bolero ranchero* as 1-rest-3-4. The *bolero* rhythm was ideally suited for popular, somewhat reserved ballroom dancing, with its simple, slow-quick-quick dance step coinciding with the bass pattern.

In 1949, the mariachi became linked to the *bolero* forever in the popular mind, and the *bolero ranchero* was born. Megastar actor/singer Pedro Infante recorded the song "Amorcito Corazón / Dear Little Heart" to the accompaniment of his mariachi, led by Juan Güitrón. This innovation, along with the efforts over the following years of Mariachi Vargas arranger Rubén Fuentes to arrange the *bolero* for mariachi, launched decades of *bolero ranchero* recordings, with certain artists, such as Javier Solís, making them their specialty. The *bolero ranchero* took the suave, romantic singing of its predecessor and cast it in a mariachi frame. The characteristic *armonía* pattern is shown in Figure 2.11.

ACTIVITY 2.10

To familiarize yourself with the bolero ranchero armonía, *listen to CD track 13, an excerpt of the* armonía *portion of the* bolero ranchero *"Si Nos Dejan / If They Let Us." Follow the pattern in Figure 2.11 until it is easy to hear. CD track 14 gives you the full instrumentation. Follow the characteristic* armonía *pattern in it as well, and notice how it gives a different feel to the piece, compared to that of the* canción ranchera *on CD tracks 3 and 12.*

The Huapango.   The *huapango* was among the mix of musical styles that arrived with the enormous migration of people from many regions of Mexico to Mexico City in the 1940s and 1950s. From the Huasteca region, overlapping the northeastern states of Veracruz, Tamaulipas, Hidalgo, San Luis Potosí, Puebla, and Querétaro, the *huapango* was marked by three traits: a distinctive rhythm, a focus on often ornate violin playing as the lead melodic instrument, and the use of the vocal falsetto to adorn the melodies.

FIGURE 2.11   *Notation of* armonía *rhythm pattern for* bolero ranchero.

A few Huastecan musician-composers, Nicandro Castillo in particular, were successful in creating a style of *huapango* that appealed to urban audiences. José Alfredo Jiménez, who in the 1950s and 1960s wrote hundreds of successful songs to be accompanied by mariachi, composed many *huapangos* that continue to be standards in the mariachi repertoire.

ACTIVITY 2.11
CD tracks 15 and 16 feature Mariachi Los Amigos performing one of José Alfredo Jiménez's most popular huapangos, "Serenata Huasteca / Huastecan Serenade." Track 15 is of the armonía section only, spotlighting the special rhythmic nucleus of the mariachi huapango. Track 16 offers the complete version. The violin introduction evokes the prominence of the violin in the regional huapango style.

The Polka. The final essential mariachi form you will learn about is the polka (sometimes spelled *polca*, in Spanish). The polka was popular in Europe in the late 1800s, and its popularity spread to Mexico. Mexican composers created their own polkas, some of which became popular in Mexico's urban dance halls and parlors. Polka ultimately came to be an important genre of the mariachi repertoire, particularly after the much-admired Mariachi México de Pepe Villa made numerous polka recordings. Other influential mariachis, such as Mariachi Vargas de Tecalitlán and Mariachi Oro y Plata, also made polka recordings, assuring the the polka's place in mariachi performances.

The rhythm of the polka is simple: 1, 2, 1, 2, 1, 2, with the *guitarrón* playing on 1 and the *vihuela* and guitar on 2. The melody is usually entirely instrumental, no vocals. The standard structure of the polka (after a short introduction) is *aabaccdcaba*, with each letter representing a sixteen-measure section of melody.

ACTIVITY 2.12
Listen to the rendition of the famous Mexican polka "Jesusita en Chihuahua" on CD track 2 and try to follow the polka struc-

ture. When you hear the melody change, make note of it. You may want to use the counter on your CD player to indicate when each new section begins. Then see if your pattern is the same as the one above. Or, simply follow along with the pattern and see how it matches up with the changes of melody in the polka.

These several genres discussed above are by no means the extent of the mariachi repertoire but are core forms among many that the mariachi plays. In fact, since these forms were in place in the 1950s, the mariachi repertoire has been ever expanding, as mariachi arrangers create versions of pieces as diverse as Venezuelan *joropos*, Broadway show tunes such as "New York, New York," the *William Tell Overture*, the country fiddle hoedown "The Orange Blossom Special," and many more.

The establishment of the basic mariachi sound in the 1950s does not mean that the sound texture has not continued to evolve. Mariachi arrangers have proliferated, and they are constantly experimenting with new rhythms, harmonies, sounds, and forms. The giant among them has been Rubén Fuentes, who joined Mariachi Vargas in 1944 and today is the group's overall director.

Mariachi Vargas music director Pepe Martínez offers his perspective on the evolution of the modern mariachi since the 1950s, noting particularly its integration of symphonic instrumentation:

In the past forty years, the evolutions have been great. I think that of those who have had much responsibility for that, for the evolutions, the principal one is Rubén Fuentes. He started, like around 1950, more or less, started an evolution of the *bolero ranchero* with Pedro Infante, and continued with Miguel Aceves Mejía with the *huapangos*. Then, . . . there was high-quality mixture that still [is]. We were commenting one time that there are a few numbers that Rubén did in 1960 that still in 1980 were difficult for the people to manage, because of the quality, that is to say, "Qué Bonita Es Mi Tierra / How Pretty Is My Land," or the *huapangos*, "La Malagueña," and all those, "La Noche y Tú / The Night and You." That type of instrumentation that he used for the first time, some violas, some cellos, some flutes, the French horns. . . . He used almost all the instruments of the symphony. Because when they started to record the music of Jorge Negrete in 1945,

FIGURE 2.12 *Composer, arranger, and artistic director of the influential Mariachi Vargas de Tecalitlán, Rubén Fuentes (on the right) has played a major role in shaping the mariachi sound ever since he joined Mariachi Vargas in the 1940s as a violinist. He poses with author backstage in Guadalajara's Teatro Degollado during the annual Encuentro de Mariachis. (Photograph by author, assisted by Alberto Alfaro, 2001)*

or 1946, around then, the one who was supervising all that was the maestro Manuel Esperón. And Rubén Fuentes was at Maestro Manuel Esperón's side, helping Maestro Esperón arrange the mariachi for Jorge Negrete. So, he was arranging for the mariachi, and they were putting the symphony over the numbers. For the films, exclusively for the films. So, that idea that is happening right now [the mariachi recording with symphony orchestra], happened before, but a complete recording was never made with mariachi and symphony. There was always only one number or two like that, and much less than now that Vargas has its first symphonic CD, now, yes, with a symphony accompanied by and using the voices and all of Mariachi Vargas. It is, now yes, it is one of the dreams, of the many dreams that I have fulfilled with him. (Martínez interview)

Many groups, especially those who regularly concertize for large audiences, have developed new arrangements of their own that take the

basic ingredients of the modern mariachi and cast them in a more contemporary style, injecting rhythms and harmonies borrowed from the
latest sounds of pop music.

ACTIVITY 2.13

Listen to CD track 17, the bolero *"Gema / Gem" by Mari-*
achi Los Camperos. Can you hear how the harmonies are com-
plex, how the arrangement goes beyond merely accompanying a
soloist, and how finely honed the precision of the performance is?

In tracing the creation of the modern mariachi sound, you have already
learned something about how social and economic dimensions affected
the evolution of the music itself. In the next chapter, I will focus on music as part of a larger fabric of social life, exploring how its meaning
and substance are closely connected to the values of the people who
perform and appreciate it.

CHAPTER 3

The Social Life of Mariachi Music

*I lived following my father . . . and grandfather around, and, obviously, I
learned from them. I remember, I already knew how to read, in the cantinas
. . . I would see the signs at the entrance that would say, "Women,
uniformed personnel, beggars, street vendors, mariachis, and dogs not
allowed." At the time, I was simply the boy of the group. They sent me
around to offer music to the tourists and clients in the cantinas. So you see, I
had to walk across the room to get to where the clients were. And before
getting to the middle of the room, they would say, "No, no, no, no! Get out
of here, get out of here!" And well, that became deeply, deeply, deeply
engraved in my mind. . . . [I was] eight years old.*
—Natividad Cano, director of Mariachi Los Camperos, recounting a memory of his childhood in Guadalajara.

THE SOCIAL DIMENSION

Mariachi music, like all music performed by people for people, has
meaning that is social and personal as well as musical. Eight-year-old
Natividad Cano learned of mariachi's low social status the hard way
when he was growing up in the 1940s, playing the music of rural la-
borers for city audiences who considered them and their music "back-
ward." The occasion, purpose, and setting imbue a performance with
special meaning. A cantina setting on a Saturday night, for example,
will call for a mood and repertoire of music much different from those
of a Mass celebration in a church on a Sunday morning. Clearly, musical sound is closely tied to social context and meaning. Music is not
purely a product of its context, however. An adept, creative musician
might make it a dynamic force that shapes social life as well as being a
reaction to it, a vehicle to express a particular meaning, to make a social statement as well as an artistic one. The message may have to do
with personal emotions—love, longing, disdain, joy, anger, or pride, for
example. Or, for instance, if a group as a whole suffers from social or

racial discrimination or is in a disadvantageous social position, music might be used to celebrate that group's identity. Or it might be used to change social values by repositioning a musical expression to a higher social status.

As mariachi music was transformed through urbanization and commercialization in the twentieth century, the variety and complexity of its social meaning greatly increased. As it moved to the United States, it attracted performers and audiences from a wider range of social groups, became a component of new performance occasions and places, and acquired even more shades of social meaning. The range of socially determined meaning of mariachi music can be very complex and can depend on a multiplicity of factors. Keeping this in mind, looking at the special meaning given mariachi music as it migrated from Mexico to the United States offers insights into how mariachi musical culture has both shaped, and has been shaped by, the communities of which it is an expression.

Nati Cano's Dream. Natividad "Nati" Cano, for decades a powerful force in the shaping of mariachi music on both sides of the United States–Mexico border, is acutely aware of the complex social evaluation of mariachi music. In his work, he has been one of the most influential mariachi musicians in engaging social issues surrounding mariachi music. When he told the story that opens this chapter, he meant for it to illustrate one of his earliest and most painful memories of social attitudes that placed the mariachi musician and mariachi music near the bottom of the social ladder. It also helps explain his motivation over most of his life to change the way people think about mariachi music.

In an interview in 1999, Cano recounted how the social position of mariachi music affected him and how he in turn shaped the music and became a force for social, as well as musical, change.

> The musicians of the symphony, the philharmonic, saw us as musicians and music that weren't worth anything, right? . . . So, they looked down on us like that, and it hurt me very much because I adored, and I still very much adore, mariachi music. Ironic, because [years later the symphony musicians] in New York in Lincoln Center told us, "This music is very difficult! It's very pretty!" Then, supposedly to rid myself of that . . . curse, I started to study classical music. I was eight or nine years old. . . . Then I started to play with a group, at about the age of ten, with a classical music group, a quartet. . . . People requested music, let's say such as *La Traviata* or *Rigoletto*. . . . They hired us to play house parties. . . . And around then I started to have

more maturity, more maturity in learning. It served me well . . . because that was the combination of being able to absorb the two musical cultures, and the one helped me with the other.

Cano's musician skills landed him a job in Guadalajara playing with a modern-style nightclub group with three violins and a string bass. "That's where I started. . . . [The group] was called Los Mensajeros 'The Messengers'. I'm talking about 1950, 1949." He was recruited to join a mariachi in Mexicali, a northern Mexican town on the border with California. "My father didn't want me to go, but my mother knew me . . . and said to him, 'You know what? You had better give him your bless-

FIGURE 3.1   *Nati Cano, founder and director of Mariachi Los Camperos, at the ¡Viva el Mariachi! Festival in Fresno, California.*   (Photograph by author, 1999)

ing, because I know that he is going to go anyway.'" His real goal was to get to Los Angeles, something he had dreamt about since the time of the social insults of his boyhood. He became the artistic director of the group in Mexicali, called Mariachi Chapala, named after the beautiful lake and town outside Guadalajara. "Unfortunately, it was a group . . . that didn't have ambition. . . . and I came along with my motor running." In 1957, Mariachi Chapala accepted an engagement at the Granada Lounge near downtown Los Angeles.

Nati's dream of reaching Los Angeles came true, but his dreams for the mariachi were far from realized.

> I had a tremendous musical ambition. . . . I knew the mariachi could be much more than it was. . . . What I didn't like was that we had to be there playing, if the people put a dollar in the kitty that we had there . . . , we had to play the song they requested. And at times we had to play the same song five times. I didn't like that. . . . We were like, pardon the expression, like prostitutes there. We couldn't enjoy the music artistically, because we had to respond to a purchase, buy and sell, buy and sell. . . . And I had problems in the Mariachi Chapala because they gave us chairs, and we played sitting down. . . . The people were dancing and were not looking at the mariachi. . . . and I would say, "No, stand up. The mariachi should be standing up." I never played sitting down, never. You only play sitting down in the symphony. The mariachi should not play sitting down. . . . So I was very discontented, because of the lack of aggressiveness, lack of a challenge, something better. It was a sameness, a weekly salary that had no incentive at all. It had no artistic pride. It was only a purchase and sale.

Greater and more prestigious frontiers beckoned that would offer him the chance to treat mariachi music as "art"—meaning having greater freedom to be creative—and to elevate its social status. "Around then the Million Dollar Theatre existed; that was the maximum. . . . The artist that played there was like—'Where are you going to sing? At the Million Dollar? 'Oh, the Million Dollar!'" Mariachi Águila was there, the house mariachi. Cano left Mariachi Chapala to join Mariachi Águila in 1961. "I was welcomed in Mariachi Águila, welcomed very well." When the group's director, José Frías, met a tragic end in a traffic accident, Nati was made the group's director. He accepted on the condition that things would change. He told them, "We have to get better; we have to be something greater, greater." With the blessing and financial backing of Frank Fouce, the Million Dollar's owner, Nati went to Mexico and purchased new uniforms. "I made a drastic change. It was the first mariachi to use the white jacket." Instead of the basic black suit commonly used by most mariachis for the sake of convenience, or even the unadorned *traje campirana* 'country-style suit', Cano created a suit of a white jacket, black pants with ornate *gala* "silver ornaments" down the side of the leg, and a fancy embroidered belt with uniform belt buckles. And, as an added touch, he often included an elegant multicolored *roana* 'blanket' draped over the shoulder. While Mariachi Vargas in Mexico for over a decade had used finely crafted outfits fitting to their involvement in the movies, such attention to appearance was the exception rather than the norm.

Cano saw the theater venue with its focus on the visual aspects of the performance as a means to raising the status of the mariachi from an anonymous background accompaniment to an upstage position as the center of attention. "I started with tricks, impact—the techniques of the stage. . . . I looked for stage colors, . . . but the white jacket had the impact! It gave it an impact of youth, of happiness, in place of somberness [of the black suit]." In addition to dress, he added a "third dimension—the choreography of the group. . . . Instead of being planted there like soldiers, we started to use movement," modest stage movement emphasizing the spirit of the song or highlighting the singer or instrument being featured. Cano also saw the "show" performance context as the vehicle to inject greater artistry into mariachi performance. He rehearsed the group three to four hours each day and insisted upon discipline, letting go musicians who would not show up for work or drank too much.

But these changes nevertheless fell short of Cano's goal—the mariachi was still subordinate to the solo artist. Mariachi Águila accompanied the top Mexican singing artists of the time, including José Alfredo Jiménez, Amalia Mendoza, Miguel Aceves Mejía, Lola Beltrán, and Javier Solís, but it was not the main attraction. Theatrical concerts showcasing mariachis did not exist on either side of the border, according to Cano. "There weren't any in Mexico. . . . Mariachi Vargas never knew it, but I followed them around . . . I learned from them. . . . But they, too, worked accompanying; they were always in second place, in back. And I, here in the United States, I started the mariachi alone [onstage]. Alone. . . . I was certain the mariachi could go independent, work by itself." What made him decide to stop accompanying artists altogether was an unfortunate occasion onstage with the renowned singer Francisco "Charro" Avitia. Avitia asked him what the next song was, and Cano checked the agreed upon list and told him what it was. "He yelled at me in an ugly way, 'No, not that one!'" Remembering how badly he had been treated as a young mariachi in Guadalajara, and feeling that the mariachi deserved greater respect, the moment pained him. He answered, "We'll play whichever one you say, then," but Avitia continued to embarrass the group, saying, "Then we won't sing." "Then we won't sing," responded Cano. The group, by now well disciplined, lowered their instruments, waiting for Avitia to decide on a song. Whistles and yells from the audience eventually brought the owner, who coaxed Avitia into continuing. The show went on, but the moment signaled a turning point for the group. With many offers to perform alone, they left the Million Dollar in 1967. Their stage savvy allowed them to get contracts playing shows, such as in Las Vegas nightclubs and on the tourist boat to Catalina Island.

The Birth of La Fonda.   Around 1965, another painful social experience added fuel to Cano's fire. Touring in Lubbock, Texas, Cano and several other members of the Camperos were refused service at a restaurant because they were Mexican.

We were with [star singer] Miguel Aceves Mejía. Clemente [the *guitarrón* player] told me, "You know that here they don't like Mexicans." "But why?" I answered. "I don't know," he said. You know, I lived in the era, right? The problem was with the African Americans, right? They didn't like them and they had to sit in the back of the bus and all that, right? But Texas? Texas had been part of Mexico. "Well, yes, but they don't like Mexicans here, and so let's not go out of the hotel." "Let's go," I said, and so we went to a restaurant and I looked inside. I saw a black man in the back washing dishes, and I said, "Well if they let him in, they will us, too." The problem was with them [the blacks], right? And when we entered—I will never forget it—a waitress, she was a white woman, saw us and just stared at us, and I said, "Uh oh." And we stood there and the headwaiter came and asked "Can we help you?" And I said, "We want to have dinner." He told me, in English, "Look, two blocks from here is a restaurant with Spanish prices." I told him, "No, I'm not asking about the prices. We're going to pay whatever you charge us." And he told me very calmly, "Look, buddy, we don't serve Mexicans." What a shock! He, not being from Mexico, where they wouldn't let [mariachis] in. The same thing [as during my youth], but in another way, in a racial way. So, we went to the hotel, and I couldn't sleep, I couldn't sleep at all. Clemente said, "Go to sleep." I told him, "No, Clemente, no. You know what? One day, I'm going to have a place where people of all colors, of all flavors, of all countries will come, come to see us." And that day, La Fonda was born.

Cano's experience with American-style racism brought up the old feelings of being discriminated against as a mariachi in Mexico. But his sleepless night and determined vow led to one of his most influential creations—La Fonda—a mariachi dinner theater featuring a mariachi show as the dinner entertainment. Cano's reaction to social and racial discrimination melded with his musical vision of treating mariachi music more as "art," not the slave of the star singer on the stage of the Million Dollar, and not beholden to the intense "buy and sell, buy and sell" of the Granada barroom.

"Around then, we were touring a lot, and I talked to [Million Dollar Theatre manager] Mr. Frank Fouce about my plans. He said, 'It's a good idea. I'll help you.' He helped me a lot. I am indebted to him a lot. . . . In those days we made good money, and we saved our money and saved our tips. It was very nice, very nice." In 1967, the eight members organized the corporation Los Camperos, Inc., from the name given the group in 1961. They leased a burnt-out building on Wilshire Boulevard, west of downtown Los Angeles, where La Fonda still stood thirty-five years later. Repairing the fire damage was expensive and daunting, and Cano remembers how "I sat down and cried in '68, right there where the stage is now." It took great confidence in the potential of the mariachi to stand alone on a stage, a confidence that was not shared by many. "Like they didn't believe in the power of mariachi music. . . . Now they do. Now everybody is an expert in [mariachi] restaurants and festivals."

When La Fonda opened in 1969, Cano resisted the pressure of the audience, accustomed to having the mariachi play whatever song they requested. "When La Fonda opened, the people came and said 'Play at my table. . . . I'll pay you. I have money.' 'No sir, I said, no. We play for everyone, so that everyone can enjoy this music.' That was the policy. That was the discipline. And it worked." Distanced from the one-on-one "buy and sell" relationship with the audience, Los Camperos played more innovative music, "absorbing other music and making it their own, and presenting it in a more elegant fashion and all. That was what drove the image of the group." They played songs like "Granada" that had broad appeal and created arrangements with featured soloists and stage movement. "It's not so much the song as it is how you present it. That's it. That's the touch that is called *guarnición* 'garnish' on a good plate of whatever it might be—meat, chicken, fish. It's the manner in which you present it."

More than thirty-five years after the opening of La Fonda, Nati Cano remains true to his vision. In La Fonda and in several other mariachi restaurants across the Southwest, the mariachi has more control over the performance space. The tyranny of "buy and sell" is not completely absent, since the musical show still needs to attract audiences for the business to be successful, but it is less intense, allowing the musicians more creative control over their performance. Cano's emphasis on discipline, attention to staging techniques and elegant uniforms, and musical independence has brought the mariachi more of the *social*, as well as artistic, recognition he sought. Los Camperos have played dozens of major concert halls for audiences in the thousands—the Kennedy Center, New York's Lincoln Center, the White House. But none of these prestigious venues was more personally satisfying than starring in Guadalajara's ornate opera house, Teatro Degollado. Guadalajara's most elegant stage is only blocks from the cantinas where in Cano's youth, "women, uniformed personnel, beggars, street vendors, mariachis, and dogs" were not allowed.

FIGURE 3.2 *La Fonda de Los Camperos Restaurant, founded in 1969 at 2501 Wilshire Boulevard in Los Angeles, California.* (Photograph by author, 1999)

FIGURE 3.3 *Nati Cano's Mariachi Los Camperos performs onstage inside La Fonda Restaurant in Los Angeles.* *(Photograph by author, 2001)*

ACTIVITY 3.1

Pick three very different kinds of music and address these questions about them in an essay. Who plays them? Who listens to them? Are they more closely linked to certain social groups, such as young people, older people, affluent people, rural people, people of a certain ethnic background, and so forth? Are any of them thought of as "art music" or "folk music"? Why or why not? What social groupings do you belong to? Are these musics that your group likes or dislikes? Why? Now do the same for mariachi music, evaluating it from your own perspective and comparing it to the perspectives of others.

Social Dimensions of Mariachi Meaning. Nati Cano's quest for greater respect for the mariachi paralleled other events in American social life. Mariachi music had been a visible part of Mexican-American life since at least the late 1930s. In 1936, the film *Allá en el Rancho Grande* and its *comedia ranchera* 'country comedy' successors were screened in Spanish-language cinemas in the United States. In fact, many of these films were more popular outside Mexico, generating profits that drove filmmakers to create more films and to distribute them in the United States. Moreover, United States–based mariachi groups accompanied touring vocalists. Singer and composer Carmencristina Moreno of Fresno, California, recalls her father's mariachi group that accompanied pioneering *ranchera* singer Lucha Reyes in Los Angeles theaters in the early 1940s: "When stars from Mexico would come over, if the budget allowed, if they wanted a bigger group, Frank [Fouce] would tell my father "get a mariachi together, get five together," and my father would organize mariachis to accompany these stars. They did that with Lucha Reyes and with a few other stars" (Moreno interview 2002).

FIGURE 3.4   *Mariachi Moreno performs onstage with legendary Mexican vocalist Lucha Reyes at the Mason Theatre in Los Angeles, 1941. Luis M. Moreno (playing* vihuela*) assembled the mariachi for the special occasion and included his wife, Carmen Moreno, playing guitar in the group. The Dueto Los Moreno was well known in the Mexican community of Los Angeles at the time.*   (Used with permission from the archives of El Dueto Los Moreno and Carmencristina Moreno)

Immigration from Mexico increased dramatically in the post–World War II years, bringing a greater demand for Mexican entertainment. By the time Los Camperos were launching their restaurant in the 1960s, a new generation of Mexican Americans had emerged. Also, the Chicano movement of the late 1960s and 1970s, following in the image of the civil rights movement for African Americans, intensified the meaning of mariachi music as a cultural symbol and as a means of cultural pride and resistance.

Mexican-American violinist Leonor Pérez (Figure 3.5), who grew up in East Los Angeles during this time, remembers the social meaning

FIGURE 3.5   *Mariachi musician and educator Dr. Leonor Xóchitl Pérez (first row, second from left), from Los Angeles, performed with the all-female Mariachi Mujer Dos Mil. Also featured are music director Laura Sobrino (second row, second from left) and director/founder Marisa Orduño (second row, third from left).*   (Used with permission from Marisa Orduño, director and founder of Mariachi Mujer Dos Mil)

mariachi music had for her, and the meaning that she put into it, during that era.

> The music that you grow up with becomes a kind of trigger for associations with your family, with your community, with the things that you see every day, . . . a trigger and a mirror back to me about what I was living at the time. And, it's interesting because, although it could have just been a trigger and a mirror back to me, I counter-reflected what I saw by inserting in it something—I added something to that reflection, by playing back into the music, what I was feeling at the time. . . . East L.A. is a very interesting place to grow up in, because it's very hard, a very hard kind of community to grow up in—there are gangs in the community. It's not exactly the safest place to grow up in (Pérez interview).

Pérez remembers the poverty and pain of growing up in East Los Angeles, but she also remembers the beauty of the people coming together to help one another as well. For her, the music offered a way to express these memories and feelings.

> I think the music talks a lot about the heartbreak and about the pain. I think the tones express that. I think the different styles. First of all, it's a vehicle to express this pain—although, we were so happy to be giving, and to be collaborative, and to be there for the community. It's also painful to see all these people in need, you know. But you have to hold up, and you don't even think about it. It's at a very subconscious level, but there's kind of a growing pain there. And you know, when you play mariachi music, it's just such a place to express, you know, to really vent and to just kind of release a lot of that that's in you. I think that mariachi music and the style of the music really provides for that to happen. So that's as a vehicle, but the music itself speaks of many of those pains. Mainly love, in the *boleros*, but of the losses and the pain, and that kind of thing. . . . For me personally, it's very closely associated with how I grew up, and what I grew up with, and what it reminds me of.

Leonor Pérez tells us something essential to understanding music: the meaning of music is not one-dimensional and absolute, rather, it is situational and depends mainly on its context and the meaning each person brings to it. The emotion one feels in singing, playing, or listening to a romantic *bolero*, for example, may connect more to one's own feelings of love or joy than the literal meaning in the words of the song. That is, the meaning of the lyrics is poetic, not just literal, evoking a higher or deeper level of feeling. For her, the music taps the wellspring of memory about the pain and joy in her life as well as her feelings of closeness to her Mexican community. For someone else, or under different circumstances, the same music might call up more literal feelings about a lost love or about the joy of being in love in general. The musical performance is like a drama in which the music triggers emotions and into which the musician "counter-reflects" and channels his or her emotions. The actual meaning of a song for the musician or the listener may be quite different from the literal meaning of a song's lyrics. Knowing that the meaning of music is situational helps us grasp how mariachi music can be a statement of social identity.

From her own experiential perspective, Pérez felt that in the United States, mariachi musicians enjoyed a privileged social status among Mexican Americans, who valued the connection of mariachi music to the cultural heritage that set them apart from others:

> Mariachis in the United States are much more accepted than in Mexico. . . . I think that in the United States we have . . . sort of a hierarchy, of varieties, of types of groups that there are, and there's a place for just about everyone. And regardless of where you are, at the very bottom is the only place where you are going to find . . . where people are not as accepting, a little bit of rejection. And at that very bottom are the Mexican immigrants who were the ones who were playing originally back in the sixties and seventies when I started.

ACTIVITY 3.2
Choose a song that has special meaning to you. Write a statement about its meaning to you. Is the meaning literally described by the song, or is it a special meaning that it has especially for you?

Pick a second song, such as "The Star-Spangled Banner," to use as a springboard for thinking about special meanings it might have for different people, including yourself.

José Hernández's Motivation. José Hernández is the director of the prominent mariachi Sol de México, a skilled music arranger, and the son of the late Esteban Hernández, a member of Mariachi Chapala with

Nati Cano in the 1950s. José has favored innovation in mariachi arranging and repertoire. Born in Mexico, when growing up in the United States, he considered himself *mexicano* more than Mexican American, and his experience growing up in the Los Angeles Mexican-American community reflects Leonor Pérez's observation about immigrant musicians located at the "bottom" of the social hierarchy in the minds of many. Hernández explained how, in his extra-musical life, being placed in this social position shaped his musical creativity.

> The way that I approach mariachi is that, I mean the soul of the music, I feel that I feel it, I mean, it's deeply rooted in me. You know, there's no other music in my heart more than mariachi. But, I grew up always having to prove myself because I was *mexicano*, not Mexican American. . . . So that had a lot to do with my music. When I arranged mariachi, I would always do other stuff from other genres and put it in the mari-

FIGURE 3.6 *José Hernández (left) founded and directs Los Angeles–based Mariachi Sol de México, one of the most popular and influential among the leading mariachi groups. In addition to his role as a bandleader, Hernández is known for his creative abilities as a composer and arranger and his skill as a performer and teacher of mariachi-style trumpet.* (Used with permission from José Hernández and Mariachi Sol de México)

achi to say, "Here, we could do it. Just as good as you could, but only with the mariachi instruments." That's what's behind my thinking when I do it. But then, like the Natis, even Rubén [Fuentes, longtime musical director of Mariachi Vargas], I mean people like that, they don't realize it. They don't, they [say], "Ah you're breaking tradition." They don't see it, that it's part of my upbringing. You understand what I mean? Twenty years ago I was writing symphonic arrangements. And, one day I'm . . . going [to compose] . . . a symphony. And it wasn't until around twelve, thirteen years [ago] that I started to direct symphony orchestras doing my music. But, it's that, you know, . . . I always feel like I have to prove myself to say, "You know what? The Mexican, yes, can do it too, you know?" And dressed up in a charro suit, directing a symphony. And something that I really do appreciate is that in Jalisco, when you go to the [mariachi] gatherings, the symphony, always the conductor conducts with the mariachi. But with me, when I go with the symphony, they have me conduct, 'because they know I personally have orchestrated my music.' There is a really nice respect, and that makes me feel really good, because I feel like I'm not using any ghostwriter. I have to prove I could do it myself.

Hernández has included the Beach Boys on one of his albums, arranged repertoire such as "New York, New York" for his Mariachi Sol de México (1997), recorded the medley "Recordando a Glenn Miller" (Remembering Glenn Miller) (1996), and made other similar artistic excursions. While some mariachi musicians feel he has stepped outside the boundaries of music that they consider to be within mariachi—or even Hispanic—tradition, he feels his contemporary arranging style is directly connected to the larger mariachi tradition rather than a "crossover" to mainstream American popular music. He also sees the social value in "proving the point" that the mariachi is a musical vehicle befitting the American mainstream: "I like to push the envelope, too, you know? But for me, it is a continuation of the school of Rubén [Fuentes], and the school of Manuel Esperón, the school of [Chucho] Ferrer, who has arranged a lot for Vargas. . . . You know, those guys have really taken risks, but they never lost the *sabor del pueblo* [taste of the people]."

ACTIVITY 3.3

Listen to CD track 18, the canción ranchera *"La Malagrade-cida" ("The Ungrateful Woman," about disappointment in love), performed by José Hernández and his Mariachi Sol de México. Hernández is an active composer, and the melody, lyrics, and arrangement are all his own. While the recording is original in all these aspects, does it retain the "mariachi sound" in the instruments, meters, rhythms, and structure of the* canción ranchera?

THE VALUE OF TRADITION

Why would someone be concerned with whether mariachi music is following tradition? If it is good music, what does it matter? Surely, one reason is the importance of mariachi music to feeling and expressing Mexican identity. In the multicultural United States society, where the connections between race, ethnicity, and social hierarchy result in social alienation felt by Mexicans and Mexican Americans, mariachi music takes on a dimension of value necessarily different from that in Mexican society. José Hernández shares a vivid memory that makes the point.

> It's the flag, brother. It's, it's, really, where we stand, it's like waving the Mexican flag. The mariachi is the flag wherever it goes. The other day we were going to go play at the Arrowhead Prom for a *rock en español* [Spanish-language rock] group called the Jaguares. These guys are phenomenal. They had 14,000 people there. And as a surprise, they asked us to end the show. When they finished their last encore, you know, they took the *bandera mexicana* [Mexican flag], they took the *bandera*, and people starting going "Booooo," and we came out. The people went crazy. The mariachi is almost more of a force than the Mexican flag. . . . Really, it's a sense of pride. . . . I mean, they actually feel that, feel what I've always felt since I was a kid. Before, they were here, "Ahaa, my grandma plays that," you know.

Hernández saw mariachi music's social value increase dramatically among Mexican Americans when popular singer Linda Ronstadt, of Mexican-American background, launched her national tour and *Canciones de Mi Padre* album in 1987. She brought a new spotlight of public attention to the music and made it "cool" to like mariachi music. Ronstadt's promotion of the music put it in a new social light—it was worthy of the American popular mainstream, not marginal, and it was contemporary, not outmoded—and Mexican Americans flocked to it. Hernández spoke of Mexican Americans who were emboldened by the popularity of Ronstadt's interpretations of classic *música ranchera*. "The best thing that ever happened to them was Linda Ronstadt, when we did that first album with her—with quite a few mariachis." Vicki Carr, also Mexican American, had popularized Mexican *música ranchera* in the 1960s, and Hernández's family was with her when she did so. "What Vicki Carr would always say with great pride was that she was Mexican. In '67 when she would go to Reno and Lake Tahoe, she took with her Mariachi Los Galleros. They were still Los Gallos, not Los Galleros, but with [my brother] Pedro and my father. Pedro would sing with Vicki."

It was the commercial popularity even more than the Chicano movement of the sixties and seventies that raised the social profile of mariachi music.

> Author's interview question to Hernández: "So you think the main force behind this greater popularization was the commercial popularity?"
> Answer: "Yes, definitely. When it became cool. . . . That's what made it cool, yeah. . . . Seeing her [Linda Ronstadt] on *Saturday Night Live* and seeing her with David Letterman." (Hernández interview)

José Hernández saw a marked increase in his restaurant business, the mariachi nightclub named Cielito Lindo.

> It made a total positive impact. Total, total, total, total. I remember musically, I wasn't too happy about it because I'm not the type of person that follows fads. And to me, when we recorded Linda Ronstadt's album, that's what she wanted, you know? It was okay. It was a very traditional record. And even Rubén [Fuentes], Rubén told me, "All these years that I have been fighting to bring mariachi, you know, forward—here we go back another forty years. . . ." When I was in high school, it wasn't all that cool to be a mariachi. You now, I was like, I was in China, I was playing other music also, but, in the seventies still, you know, it was okay. There was El Rey [his brother's mariachi nightclub], there was La Fonda, and when we were in school it wasn't cool, but now, you know, to have it in the schools and to have it such a big sort of program! (Hernández interview)

Sentiments about the special appreciation of mariachi music and musicians by the American public have also been echoed by Mexican-

American brothers Randy and Steve Carrillo, who helped found Mariachi Cobre in Tucson, Arizona, in 1971 and have performed with the group at Epcot Center in Orlando, Florida, since 1982. When Steve visited Mariachi Vargas in Mexico, the group he idolized, in the late 1980s, he was taken aback by how the group was treated by the public there. He characterized the attitude as "Oh, mariachis—another plain-old mariachi type of thing. In the United States, when we were growing up, you know, Vargas—wow!" Randy adds: "We held them in a different esteem, and they weren't treated [in Mexico] the way you thought they should have been treated."

Fellow Cobre member Héctor Gama, who was raised in Mexico, feels that popular films have shaped the public's behavior toward mariachi musicians. "For example, [actor/singer] Pedro Infante won over the

FIGURE 3.7 *Mariachi Cobre, founded in Tucson, Arizona, has performed regularly at Epcot Center in Orlando, Florida, since 1982. Guitarronero (guitarrón player) Randy Carrillo, trumpeter Steve Carrillo and arranger Frank Grijalva are fourth, fifth, and sixth from the left in the second row. Héctor Gama is third from the left in the first row.* (Used with permission of Randy Carrillo and Mariachi Cobre)

public a lot because he played personalities of regular people, of the common folk, of people of the humblest means. That was a noble accomplishment of his career, but at the same time it influenced people around the world in that many people believe that we still talk like that." Gama underscores the point that the exaggerated or parodied attitudes of country people toward mariachi musicians as portrayed in films took on a reality of their own and undermined respect for mariachis as accomplished music professionals.

WOMEN IN THE MARIACHI

Mariachi music reflects and projects other social meanings, such as those surrounding gender. Until mariachi music became well established in the United States, women rarely took active roles as professional mariachi musicians. With the exception of the female soloists they accompanied, mariachi performance was a male domain. None of the well-known groups included women as fellow musicians. Social limits in the United States, however, were not so restrictive, especially as the women's liberation movement gained momentum.

Rebecca Gonzales: Opening the Way for Women in the Mariachi. In the 1970s, several women entered the ranks of leading mariachis, igniting a lasting trend. The first of these was violinist and singer Rebecca Gonzales. Born and raised in San Jose, California, Gonzales studied violin in public school and had hopes of being a professional musician. While a student at San José City College in 1972, she attended a recently launched mariachi performance class, taught by Mark Fogelquist, a graduate of UCLA's mariachi program and director of Mariachi Uclatlán in Los Angeles. The attraction of the music was strong. She began to play with a local mariachi in a humble Mexican bar, with the approval of her father, a friend of the owner. Her repertoire grew, and when Fogelquist invited her to join Mariachi Uclatlán, she accepted. In Los Angeles, the presence of a woman in a successful mariachi attracted attention, and her notoriety spread. As her determination to make a career of mariachi music grew, she set her eyes on the most prestigious group around, Nati Cano's Mariachi Los Camperos. She often visited Cano's restaurant, La Fonda. Her reputation had preceded her, and one day Cano invited her to join Los Camperos.

Gonzales recalls some friction with social gender boundaries after she began playing with Mariachi Los Camperos. She felt a tension, a

FIGURE 3.8 *Rebecca Gonzales (center) is pictured with Mariachi Uclatlán, circa 1974, before she joined Mariachi Los Camperos. Group director Mark Fogelquist is third from the left, author is fourth from left.* (Used with permission from Mark Fogelquist, director, Mariachi Uclatlán)

look of discomfort on the faces of some of the older men when she was playing or singing.

> Maybe it wasn't so much that they didn't like it, maybe it was more a feeling of you know, the difference, the fact that there was a woman now here, instead of a man being next to them. . . . Imagine, these men, probably been playing all their lives, and all of a sudden, there's a woman there next to them, and it's just sort of a feeling of, this is sort of bizarre. Maybe [it was] that kind of feeling more than anything else, because they were kind to me. That's why I don't think it was that they didn't like me. It was more, this is bizarre. . . . I remember it was . . . maybe a month at the most, at the very most, and then all of a sudden, I felt this air of relaxation, you know, all of a sudden I was playing, and now this feeling of tension in the air was no longer there and I felt like we were one. . . . It was like playing

with women or something. It didn't feel any different. (Gonzales interview)

Laura Sobrino: The Challenge of Change. Rebecca's success emboldened other women to become professional mariachi musicians, and, since it was proven to make good business sense, it was easier for other group leaders to follow suit and invite women to join them. Laura Sobrino joined Mariachi Los Galleros in Los Angeles, a rival group to Los Camperos. Sobrino had similar experiences along the fault line between older social standards that excluded women and her presence in the mariachi, such as men treating her like someone to dance with rather than a musician to listen to. At the same time, she sees the lasting change

FIGURE 3.9 *Laura Sobrino performs onstage with Mariachi Mujer Dos Mil in Fresno's Convention Center during the ¡Viva el Mariachi! Festival.* (Photograph by author, 2001)

that has resulted. As to the future of women in mariachi music in the United States, she is optimistic.

I think the doors are open for them, I think people have accepted it, at least now. It still amazes me that twenty five years after playing, . . . twenty years in L.A., . . . people still look at me and say, "It's so nice to see a woman playing mariachi. . . . How long have you been doing this?" . . . That [it's still a novelty] irritates me a lot, especially after going through what I went through, you know, for so many years. Okay, it's not good enough just to know second violin, you have to know first violin, third violin; you have to know how to sing! Ah! You know? Or you have to have physical stamina, you have to know how to deal with customers who think you are up here to sell your body and not to play music. All those things, they are going to have to deal with at an individual level. (Sobrino interview)

ACTIVITY 3.4
Listen carefully to CD track 19, "Tema Mujer 2000," com-posed by Pepe Martínez and given to the all-female group Mari-achi Mujer Dos Mil as their theme to open performances. Other than the singers' voices being those of women rather than men, can you hear any difference in the overall sound or quality of per-formance from the all-male mariachis featured on the CD?

ACTIVITY 3.5
Up to this point in the book, you have been introduced to a num-ber of mariachi groups, in terms of their music, their leaders, and their experiences. Collate all you have learned about each group from reading, listening, and lectures. Then make a comparative chart, to put them in perspective with each other.

Step 1. Sort all the collated information in this way: analyze the types of information you have, for example, whether they are Mexican or Mexican American, and where in either place their base is, any specialization within mariachi repertoire, what their ideas about mariachi tradition are, their main professional activ-

ities, the significance (or not) of their leader, and other types of information.

Step 2. Structure your chart. On paper or in your computer list all the types of information (parameters) down the left side, and all the groups across the top (or vice versa). Create columns and boxes to fill in with your collated information.

Step 3. Fill in the four boxes. You will find that you must leave some empty, and that is fine.

From the chart, extract—write up—two points about mariachi that you consider to be most interesting and significant.

Mariachi music has a rich social life, filled with different shades of meaning for those who practice it and appreciate it. For some, the music is a source of social grounding, a music that makes them feel "at home" when they listen to it. For others, it is an agent for social change and way of asserting their presence in a multicultural society, saying "Here I am, and my culture is great." Or it is both. The same music can have different meanings for different people in different social settings. As the particular musicians, audiences, performance occasions, kind of music, purpose of the performance, or place of the performance changes, the meaning of the music may change along with it. Individual musicians may approach music making from a variety of perspectives and motivations. Musicians and audiences all are members of larger social groups, and they bring the values and perspectives of these groups to bear on the performance context. In the next chapter, I will focus on how being a professional mariachi musician in Mexico and the United States defines an occupation and a subcultural group with a unique economic life.

CHAPTER 4

Mariachi Economy: *Al Talón, Chambas, Plantas*, Shows, and *La Mariachada*

A recent college graduate was telling his girlfriend, her sister, and my son César how excited he was because he just got a salary increase. "How much do they pay you?" the girlfriend asked him. "One hundred twenty pesos per week," he answered. And then it occurred to her to ask César, "How much do they pay you?" "Sometimes I make 1000, sometimes I make 1500—800 at the lowest." "What? What, what, what do you do?" the fellow stuttered.

—Musician Margarito Gutiérrez recalls a street corner conversation in
Guadalajara with his mariachi musician son, César.

MARIACHI AS A PRODUCT AND A PROFESSION

Mariachi music is a commodity. It is bought and sold. In Chapter 3, Nati Cano lamented the sometimes demeaning "buy and sell" atmosphere of the Granada nightclub. He felt it restricted his musical creativity and his social ambitions for mariachi music. He yearned for performance settings that not only would honor the music's artistry and bring it greater social recognition, but that also would increase possibilities for economic gain. Economic factors have long contributed to shaping the mariachi's musical repertoire and performance style, the places it is played, its image, and much more. Also, the business practices and relationships shared by professional mariachi musicians bond them together in a common occupation that in turn gives rise to social bonds as well as economic ones. Linked by a common profession, professional mariachi musicians are a community unto themselves. In this chapter I delve into how different settings for the sale of mariachi music are intertwined with what music is performed and in what fashion, and how sharing an occupation builds a sense of community among mariachi musicians.

On the one hand, mariachi musicians often have an unenviable social standing, but musicians who are proficient and enterprising can make a good living as skilled tradesmen, often earning a wage greater than that of college graduates. As mariachi violinist Margarito Gutiérrez of Guadalajara once commented, "I remember when I was young, when I was chasing girls, and when they realized that I worked as a [mariachi] musician, . . . they would say, 'That's it. No, no, no,' always 'no.' " In contrast, his account of his son César's street corner conversation that opens this chapter shows he outearned his college graduate neighbor.

Mariachi musicians have long been valued as skilled tradesmen. The first written account of mariachi musicians in 1852 proves the point. After the parish priest put an end to the music on Holy Saturday, the town mayor raised money to hire another group. From nineteenth-century documents, we can gather that mariachi musicians were hired to perform at fairs, saint's day celebrations, and other public and private events. When mariachi musicians migrated to Mexico City in the 1920s and later, they began to carve out careers as full-time paid professional musicians, something that was unlikely in the rural ranch lands of home. One of the ways that pioneering mariachi groups such as Cirilo Marmolejo's Mariachi Coculense and Concepción "Concho" Andrade's Mariachi de Concho Andrade made a living was to play in the renowned cantina El Tenampa, located in what is now Plaza Garibaldi. In doing this, these early arrivals to Mexico City launched a major tradition of mariachi musicians gathering at Plaza Garibaldi to play in the surrounding restaurants, bars, and nightclubs, or to wait for clients to come by and hire them for special events elsewhere. Today, hundreds of mariachis gather daily in Plaza Garibaldi, playing for people who visit the plaza to hire them by the song, and standing on the side of the avenue waiting for potential customers to drive up and hire them.

THE EXPANDING MARIACHI MARKET

When, beginning in the 1930s, the Mexican movie industry employed mariachis such as Mariachi Tapatío, directed by Cirilo Marmolejo's nephew José Marmolejo, as a "country" backdrop to the drama and as backup musicians to singing stars, it contributed to professionalizing

FIGURE 4.1 *For over eighty years, mariachis have gathered to offer their services at Mexico City's Plaza Garibaldi. Clients come to the plaza to hire mariachi groups for celebrations elsewhere, or they may hire them for a short* serenata *(serenade) in the plaza. In this photo, a man has hired Mariachi Jalisco to serenade his wife on her birthday.* (Photograph by author, 1997)

the mariachi in other ways. The popularity of these films through the 1940s and 1950s etched the image of the mariachi in the public mind, and the elegant, tight-cut suits and wide sombreros became part of the mariachi "product." Also, the polished, even operatically trained style of the singer/actors they accompanied had great impact on the public's expectation of their own singing style. While a *canción mexicana* 'Mexican song' vein of music-making had been important since the nineteenth century, and even though Mexican audiences had long adored opera singers from Italy and other parts of Europe, it was the influence of the cinema that made the solo singer, singing in a dramatic, bel canto style, an essential ingredient of urban professional mariachi performance. The mariachi's presence in the potent media of popular films helped establish it as an important "brand" of music to audiences throughout Mexico, opening a mariachi niche in the music mass marketplace.

The growth and importance of radio in Mexican life also helped increase the economic value of mariachi music. Shortly after the powerful station XEW took to the airwaves in 1930, the live sounds of Mariachi Tapatío and, several years later, Mariachi Vargas de Tecalitlán were heard in every corner of the country, expanding the music's demand (Clark 1994:3). In fact, the XEW signal was so powerful that its programming reached the United States and Central America, expanding foreign markets as well. Radio was a relatively inexpensive technology, more so in the 1930s and 1940s than record players, and its impact on people of all economic levels was great.

By the second half of the twentieth century, the image and style of mariachi music that was seen on the screen and heard via radio waves was widely accepted in urban areas as a key pan-Mexican form of musical entertainment. It had moved beyond where it was at the beginning of the twentieth century—a music representing a specific regional culture, a regional folk music. It had more universal appeal, and while its image was understood to represent Jalisco and the rural ranch heritage, the popular media made it clear that it was a music that belonged to all Mexicans. In economic terms, this meant that the market for mariachi music reached throughout Mexico and beyond. In fact, by the end of the century, mariachi music was enough in demand in most countries of the Western hemisphere to support full-time professional mariachi ensembles. In most Latin American countries—Colombia, Venezuela, Guatemala, Bolivia, Nicaragua, and El Salvador, to name a few—thousands of local professional musicians don the Mexican *traje de charro* 'Mexican cowboy suit' of the mariachi and hire themselves out, playing the latest *canciones rancheras*, *boleros*, or *sones* for eager customers.

Today, mariachis work in many kinds of settings, from humble bars and restaurants to birthdays and wedding celebrations to concert stages, television variety shows, and recording studios. The business of mariachi music is important both to what the music sounds like and to its social dimensions as well. You will now learn about various performance settings for mariachi music, the economic practices that go along with them, and the way these factors shape mariachi culture.

PERFORMANCE SETTINGS

Whether in Mexico or the United States, mariachi musicians find themselves in several types of professional performance situations. Each type involves a certain kind of business arrangement, favors certain skill sets, shapes the social relationship between the performers and the audience, and has a direct bearing on the repertoire and quality of music performed (Pearlman 1984).

Al Talón. One of these performance settings is known among the musicians as playing *al talón*. *Talón* in Spanish means "shoe heel," and refers to how the musicians walk from one table or bar to another ["hoofing it"], looking for people who want to hire them to play. In *talón* playing, the mariachi charges the client by the song. The customer asks for a song, establishes the price per song, and the mariachi plays it. When the customer's requests are satisfied, the mariachi collects in cash. In the United States, the price charged may range from between one to two dollars per musician per song. For example, if a six-piece group plays five songs charging six dollars per song, the mariachi will earn thirty dollars, to be divided among the six musicians. Each musician might receive one dollar per song.

Al talón is in some ways the most challenging performance situation, and at the same time, one of the most educational. Pepe Martínez, musical director of Mariachi Vargas de Tecalitlán, explained his experience playing *al talón*:

> *Al talón* playing has a lot to do with repertoire, with knowledge, with transposition, styles of arrangements, of feelings. So the musician, when he starts to play in what is the *talón*, here we call it the *kitty*, or there along the border they call it the kitty, where one plays at the tables, and "What piece would you like?" So, the public itself has its predilections, has its favorites. They say, "Play me 'Por amores como tú,' and 'Por mujeres como tú,'" and "Play 'Ella,' by José Alfredo." And all of the musicians need to know what the public asks for. I lasted ten years at the kitty, that is, the *talón*, in a restaurant in Guadalajara, some ten years, where the public told me what they wanted to hear tomorrow. "Listen, tomorrow I am going to come by and I want you to play me the song 'Sombras.'" "Well, okay, tomorrow I will have it for you." Well then, the guys would show up an hour early. I would [teach them] an easy little *adorno* 'counter melody' and the introduction, and we rehearsed it beforehand—and a one, and a two. The client would show up and say "Well?" "Here is your song," and bam. And that is a glimpse, an example that I give you, because there are people who, for lack of a single song, will not hire the mariachi [for a future engagement]. So then, up to a certain point, this can be a piece of advice for all the mariachis in the world—take the opportunity to be in the *talón* or in the kitty, or in a regular gig where you have to play for the people what the people want to hear. (Martínez interview)

The *al talón* way of working has many implications for the musicians. Most important, the musicians only get paid if they know the songs customers ask for. Obviously, being able to play a large repertoire of pieces commonly requested by mariachi fans is at a premium. Given that there are many thousands of songs and instrumental pieces that have become popular since mariachi music became widely popular in the 1930s, maintaining such a vast repertoire is challenging, and to play polished arrangements of so many tunes is impossible. To be successful in the *al talón* setting, each group must have at least one singer with a large repertoire of songs, and the group must be able to at least improvise arrangements on the spot, unless one or more of the instrumentalists can lead the others in piecing together a known arrangement from a popular recording. At a minimum, the group will play the final phrases of the vocal melody as an introduction, the singer will sing the song, and the group will end with a stock ending melody.

In the *talón* environment, standardization of certain musical elements are necessary for the musicians to meet the demands of playing the

FIGURE 4.2 *In a rare moment, an "off-duty" mariachi musician hires an impro-vised group of his comrades to play for him in an* al talón *performance setting in Café Mitla near the Plaza de los Mariachis in East Los Angeles.* (Photograph by author, 2004)

enormous repertoire of mariachi tunes. Knowledge of stock endings, countermelodies (*adornos*), and introductions are basic to mariachi playing.

A stock *de cajón* (from the drawer) *ranchera* introduction called a *sinfonía* used to be common, but its popularity has dwindled. Nevertheless, mariachi musicians need to know it, in case it is called for. From a musical point of view, then, standardized musical phrases such as these are important tools of the trade in working *al talón*.

ACTIVITY 4.1

Listen to CD examples of these stock phrases (Figure 4.3) as follows:

CD track 20 fast duple-meter ranchera *ending*

CD track 21 slow duple-meter ranchera *ending*

CD track 22 triple-meter ranchera *ending*

CD track 23 bolero ending

CD track 24 son ending *version 1*

CD track 25 son ending *version 2*

The *al talón* setting has still other implications for the performance of the music. Since the musicians are paid by the song, there is an incentive to play as many songs as possible in the time available. The instrumental introduction may be truncated, nonessential verses may be dropped, and the tempo of the music may be accelerated in order to shorten the length of each piece.

Al talón playing calls for interpersonal skills in a way that other performance settings do not. The song-by-song interaction between musicians and customer is much more intense than playing a concert from a stage for an audience seated a comfortable distance away. Mariachi musicians will do all they can to play the songs requested and to satisfy the people paying them. This can be challenging, as many customers in the rougher bars can become unpleasant and even abusive if they feel the mariachi is not doing a good job. For this reason, and to keep the mariachi playing (and earning), it helps for the musicians to be skilled at talking to the customers, keeping them content and requesting more music. Playing *al talón* can be tough in terms of the social challenges it presents.

a. Canción ranchera. Fast tempo.

b. Canción ranchera. Slow tempo.

c. Canción ranchera. Slow tempo.

d. Bolero. Moderate tempo.

e. Son. Moderate-paced, free rhythm.

f. Son. Fast tempo.

FIGURES 4.3A, B, C, D, E, AND F   *Notation of common formulaic endings for* canciones rancheras, boleros rancheros, *and* sones.

Al talón playing can also be challenging in that many customers like to do the singing, with the musicians backing them up. From a musical point of view, this can be disastrous, as amateur singers range from accomplished aficionados to total incompetents who cannot sing on pitch, in rhythm, or with the correct texts. Many *taloneros* (musicians who play *al talón*) are skilled at accompanying terrible singers, and are able to instantaneously shift meter, change key, or fill in the correct lyrics. For musicians who value good-sounding performances, this type of performing can be enormously dissatisfying and grating on the nerves. Others enjoy the game of shaping the music to fit the singer, however terrible he or she might be. In any case, the ability to accompany amateur singers can be important in attracting and keeping paying customers.

It is easy to see how the forces of economics in the *al talón* setting have a strong affect on the music played. The audience controls the repertoire. If the customer asks for the song "Guadalajara" ten times, the mariachi plays it ten times. To maximize their earnings, the musicians often sacrifice the music's integrity in order to play the most pieces in the least amount of time. The number of musicians in a group is kept to a minimum, enough (five to seven, usually) to duplicate the popular mariachi sound, but not too many to make the price per song out of reach of most customers. Economics shape the social relationship between performer and audience, as the *al talón* environment requires the musicians to relate closely with their audience. Also, since the musical emphasis is on quantity of music played rather than the polished intricacy of the performance, groups of musicians playing *al talón* most often are not well-rehearsed, organized groups, but rather improvised groups of musicians who need work and cannot find it in a better-paying, more organized mariachi.

Chambas.   *Chambas* are the Mexican equivalent of "gigs" in American English. A group is hired, usually by the hour, to play for some special celebration, such as a birthday, wedding, anniversary, baptism, or even a funeral. The client and group leader negotiate the starting time, the number of hours to be played, the number of musicians in the group, and the price. The client may have special conditions, such as requests for certain songs, wanting two trumpets in the group, limiting the amount of breaks the musicians take, and so forth. In the United States, groups may charge the equivalent of $40 to $50 per person per hour. On a late Saturday afternoon or evening, when demand is the highest, the price may be higher. On a weekday, the price may be lower. When customer and leader are in agreement, the *chamba* is set.

At the appointed time, the mariachi begins to play. At the beginning of most *chambas*, the mariachi is usually free to play the repertoire of its own choosing, as long as it fits the occasion. *Sones*, polkas, popular *canciones rancheras*, *boleros*, *huapangos*, and medleys such as those learned from recordings by Mariachi Vargas de Tecalitlán are popular possibilities. As the party-goers settle in, the alcoholic beverages begin to flow, and the enthusiasm rises, the people begin to request favorite pieces, often singing along as best they can. The musicians, of course, do their best to satisfy the requests, but while they do feel the pressure to play each request, the stress is not as intense as in the *al talón* setting. The musicians have more opportunity to perform selections they know the best or have recently rehearsed. The social event is the focus, and the listeners may prefer to talk, eat, or dance while the musicians play. This is especially true when mariachis play for audiences who are not deeply familiar with the large mariachi repertoire. Many Americans, for example, only know to ask for a few longtime favorites, such as "Cielito Lindo," "Allá en el Rancho Grande," or "La Paloma," leaving the musicians to select most of the pieces they will play. At most *chambas,* there is little pressure to play a large number of pieces, as long as the breaks between pieces played are kept to a reasonable minimum. In the United States, the musicians may take occasional breaks, included in the contracted time. The hosts might even invite them to eat along with the guests.

Unlike in the *al talón* situation, mariachi groups that play *chambas* tend to be more organized. They may be an ongoing group that rehearses regularly, or they may be specially selected musicians known for their skill, mastery of repertoire, and dependibility. Generally, more effort is put into musical skill level of these groups, partly because if the group plays well and pleases its audience, its good reputation spreads, attracting more business in the future. Word of mouth, listings in the telephone yellow pages, musical entertainment agencies, and, more recently, websites are among the means the public can use to locate mariachi groups.

ACTIVITY 4.2
Do a search in easily available sources to get a sense of whether there is a mariachi music space in your area (however you want to define that).

Consider conducting a mini field research project, if it seems feasible. You will find instruction for that in Wade's Thinking Musically *(2004), Chapter 7, in this Global Music Series.*

In Mexico and among immigrant musicians in large cities of the United States, another form of clearing house for mariachi musicians is a known gathering place where dozens or hundreds of mariachi musicians congregate. A group may agree to rendezvous there to depart for a *chamba* elsewhere, or unaffiliated musicians may gather to organize groups on the spot. The Plaza Garibaldi in Mexico City, the Placita de los Mariachis in Guadalajara, and Plaza de los Mariachis the corner of

First and Boyle Streets in East Los Angeles, for example, are well-known gathering places where mariachis wait for clients to come along. In Plaza Garibaldi, where hundreds of musicians assemble daily, catching up on the latest gossip while they wait for work, a particular mariachi may have a special whistle to signal that one of them has found a client and they should come together to play. In more recent years, beepers and cell phones have extended the reach of the whistle. In Los Angeles, where hundreds of mariachi musicians live within two or three blocks of the corner of First and Boyle, a quick call to their cell phones can bring a group together in a matter of minutes.

In the *chamba* setting, in which the musicians are paid by the hour and not by the song, there is much less intense negotiation between musician and client, and much less pressure to crank out tunes in the manner of a jukebox in overdrive. The repertoire is controlled in part by the mariachi, in part by the audience, and the performance is part show, part playing requests. The mariachi is more independent, and it is bet-

FIGURE 4.4   *Mariachis gather near the corner of First and Boyle Streets in East Los Angeles to wait for customers to come along and hire them for* chambas, *or* "gigs."   *(Photograph by author, 2004)*

ter able to perform more intricate arrangements and more polished versions of pieces. It also earns more money than playing *al talón*.

ACTIVITY 4.3

Imagine you are a mariachi musician playing for four hours straight in a setting that is al talón. *If your five-member group charges five dollars per song, and you are able to play an average of twenty songs per hour, how much would you make? Compare this to playing a four-hour* chamba *in a seven-piece group that charges $350 per hour. Write a statement saying which setting you would prefer, and why.*

Serenata. A special, popular type of *chamba* is a *serenata*, literally, a "serenade." The *serenata* tradition is a favorite in Mexican and many other Latin cultures. A man may want to impress his girlfriend, or a family may wish to surprise Mom on Mother's Day with an unexpected serenade by a mariachi. Mariachis in Mexico and the United States usually have a fixed number of songs, perhaps seven or eight, that constitute a *serenata*, lasting perhaps half an hour. For a *serenata*, they may charge slightly more than an hour's fee, taking the travel time into account. The longstanding importance of the *serenata* in Hispanic tradition adds to the mariachi's enormous popularity in many Latin American countries, such as Guatemala, El Salvador, Venezuela, Colombia, and Bolivia.

Plantas. *Plantas* are regular gigs, and the client is usually a business, such as a restaurant, hotel, theater, tourist cruise ship, and so forth. Typically, a mariachi would have a *planta* in a restaurant, playing perhaps every Friday and Saturday from 7 p.m. to 10 p.m. In some restaurants, the performance is casual, and the mariachis may stand in one spot or circulate throughout the restaurant. If the customers ask for certain songs, the musicians usually try to play them, and when they do, the customers often offer a tip, even though the musicians are paid by the establishment. In other restaurants, such as Nati Cano's La Fonda de Los Camperos in Los Angeles, the musicians perform from a stage and have a more-or-less fixed list of songs they play for a set of forty-five minutes to one hour. The setting is more like a dinner theater, where the clientele goes to eat, drink, and enjoy a good show.

In the restaurant *planta*, the mariachi's independence from the audience increases yet more than in the *chamba* situation. This is not to say that they do not try to please the audience. They do. It means that they are able to please them more on their (the musicians') terms. The business dealings are with the restaurant managers, not the audience, and the mariachi is largely free to choose the repertoire it performs. The more formal the dinner theater setting, the more the musicians are able to focus more intensely on well-rehearsed, complex arrangements. In terms of earnings, the pay varies and is often less than what a musician would make playing *chambas*. The trade-off for slightly lower pay, however, is the dependibility of having regular work. Having a *planta* or two helps keep a group together and offers regular exposure that leads to additional *chambas*. The more a group prospers, the more it stays together, and the more it stays together, the more opportunity it has to be creative in its arrangements and performances. And the more distant the musicians are from the "buy and sell" demands of individual customers, the more space they have for aesthetic creativity, the fulfillment of Nati Cano's dream.

FIGURE 4.5   *Mariachi Nuevo México plays at the customers' tables in Garduño's Mexican restaurant in Albuquerque.*   (Photograph by author, 2003)

Shows. The show setting that spotlights the mariachi, rather than having it back up marquee-name solo singers, is a relatively new—and hard-earned—phenomenon. Before the 1970s, when the mariachi performed in theatrical shows, it was mostly relegated to the role of backup group. When it was featured in the movies in the late 1930s, 1940s, and 1950s, it was almost always used as a stage prop, a backdrop to the singing superstars. With the rise of television in the 1950s, the pattern continued. Since the earliest mariachi recordings, mariachi groups made recordings featuring themselves. For example, in the 1950s, Mariachi México de Pepe Villa made solo recordings of polkas and *pasodobles,* and in 1958, Mariachi Vargas de Tecalitlán came out with their milestone recording, *El Mejor Mariachi del Mundo* (RCA 1156). In live performances, however, the mariachi was rarely featured alone, except as a warm-up group to ready the audience for the featured act.

Nati Cano saw the mariachi's potential and looked for the opportunity to place the mariachi front and center onstage, where he thought it belonged. "I was certain the mariachi could become independent, work on its own terms. That is, the mariachi was worthy, we no longer had to depend [on the soloists]." As described in Chapter 3, he started his efforts to upgrade the mariachi's onstage presence years before opening La Fonda. His account mentions three principles to make the mariachi more effective onstage: add color and vibrance to the mariachi uniforms; experiment with stage choreography; and discipline the group by rehearsing three to four hours each day. When La Fonda opened in 1968, the fourth very important principle that distinguished Cano's new mariachi dinner theater setting from previous performance venues was the policy of playing for all the people, not just for certain paying clients.

This policy gave Los Camperos the freedom to create their own arrangements, plan a show set the way they wanted, and inject a new dimension of structure and visual appeal to their performance. It was also another major step away from the "buy and sell" relationship between musician and customer that Cano had long sought to avoid. In this sense, it distanced the musicians from the audience socially for the benefit of the musical expression. It created a model that many other restaurants have followed over the years since 1969. From the point of view of the music, it meant that the mariachi could concentrate more on refining arrangements of a much smaller repertoire than that required of the *talón, chamba,* and *planta* settings. The financial success of the restaurant allowed for enviable salaries for the musicians, which led to greater long-term stability of the members and a higher level of performance. In turn, the skill required to play the refined, complex

FIGURE 4.6   *Mariachi Reyna de Los Angeles, founded by José Hernández in Los Angeles, California, was the first all-female mariachi to appear in major U.S. performance venues. They are shown onstage at the ¡Viva el Mariachi! Festival in Fresno, California.*   (Photograph by author, 2000)

arrangements meant that only highly skilled musicians were able to enter the group. And only those with the dependibility and discipline required of stage-oriented performance, in which visual appeal is as prominent as the musical product, remained.

Understanding these four performance settings, which taken together cover most of the professional performance realm of mariachi music, as well as the economic practices that go along with them elucidates the impact of economics on the creation of mariachi music. There is another twist to the economic life of mariachi music that is important to keep in mind. Mariachi musicians, who spend a lifetime of shared interests together, are a unique social group unto themselves.

LA MARIACHADA

The common lot of mariachi musicians who devote such a major part of their lives to mariachi music performance creates a shared sense of purpose and experience that bonds the musicians together as the *mari-achada*, as they call themselves. To survive and thrive, musicians depend upon each other for many essentials to making their living. They need to organize themselves into groups. They need to know the level of competence of their fellow musicians. They need to network among one another in order to find work, to get the best deals on uniforms, instruments, and music supplies, and to learn the latest gossip from the mariachi grapevine. When playing music, they need to have a common way of communicating certain critical information of their trade, such as what key to play in, what chord is next, or when a song should end. They need to have a mutual understanding as to how business will be done.

Mariachi musicians, especially first-generation immigrant mariachis whose sole livelihood is their musical craft, spend a lot of time together. Much of it is spent waiting—waiting for a customer to come along, a performance to start, a break to end, and so forth. What do they do? Talk. Pass on the latest gossip, critique other musicians and groups, recount stories about other musicians, tell jokes. Mariachi humor is intense.

They frequently have *apodos* 'nicknames' for each other, often disparaging or humorous in nature. *Apodos* are powerful signifiers that tend to capture some idiosyncracy of a person and brand him or her for life. Margarito Gutiérrez, for example, is known as Santa Claus, because of his rotund shape. He remembers how he was once playing pool in Tijuana, and a fellow musician walked in and said, "¿Qué traes, pinche Santa Claus norteamericano?" 'What's with you, you crummy North American Santa Claus?' The Santa Claus label stuck with him from then on, and more musicians know him by his *apodo* than by his legal name. *Guitarrón* player César López is known as "El Pescado" 'The Fish', because his thin lips resemble those of a fish. One musician who had an embittered side to his personality was known as "El Nube Gris" 'The Grey Cloud', also the name of a well known waltz-meter song. A mariachi musician once told me in hushed tones that a certain trumpet player who constantly puckered his lips and who had a brash sense of humor was known as "El Ano" 'The Anus'. The trumpeter was nearby, and he didn't want him to hear what everyone called him. I was once given a nickname as, well, "El Camarón" 'The Shrimp', because of the particular shade of red my face turned when playing the trumpet.

Apodos are funny, but they also serve to bind mariachi musicians together, both through insider humor and through mutually understood cultural "signposts" that mark their belonging to a special group. *Apo-*

dos are part of the social "glue" that underscores their commitment to their profession and their role in life.

Charras 'jokes' can also signify the special bonds between mariachi musicians. Good humor promotes collegiality and good morale about one's comrades. Some jokes are specific to mariachi lifestyle, further acknowledging the bonds among themselves. In one *charra*, a musician visits his *compadre*, also a musician, and his wife. When the two men go out to the corner store to buy beer, a car runs over the woman's husband. From her window, she sees her husband whisper last words into his *compadre's* ear and then die in his arms. The wife runs to his side and asks the *compadre* what her husband's last words were. He answers, "They were, they were . . . *'tan-tan.'"* "*Tan-tan*" are the syllables used to mean the last two notes of a *canción ranchera* stock ending (dominant, tonic, for you musicians). He expressed his life's end with one of the most clichéd, classic signifiers of a musical *fin*. This is a classic example of an insider joke that has special meaning for the mariachis themselves.

Shared specialized skills, a network of connections to get work, insider language about music, a common understanding of mariachi business practices, living side-by-side in urban neighborhoods of mariachi musicians, and the sheer quantity of time spent together links mariachi musicians to form a unique social subculture. For immigrant musicians living in a foreign environment, these connections, this sense of community, are all the more important. The social bonds among mariachi musicians create a distinctive social group unto itself, an occupational community that is a vital dimension of "mariachi culture."

CHAPTER 5

¡Viva el Mariachi! Tacos with Ketchup or Salsa? The Challenge of Change

You should not change things that are classic. You should leave them intact. They ask me, "How do you like this mariachi?" "How do you like that mariachi?" And I tell them, "Look, we should not all do the same thing. It is not good for humanity for everything to be the same." But there are some limits. There is a limit which says, "This just is not how it should be. It is now something else." Here is how I put it. The taco, apart from the mariachi and tequila, is the worldwide image of Mexico, right? On the taco, put salsa de tomate, salsa verde, salsa de chipotle, *put whatever salsa you like. But just don't put ketchup.*

—Nati Cano

Mariachi culture is changing. This is to be expected, because all cultures and all musics evolve over time. It is also to be expected that mariachi culture—both the music and its meaning to people in society—when transplanted to the United States, would change even more rapidly than in Mexico. Before Nati Cano created Los Camperos and La Fonda, mariachi music was a music from Mexico. It might have been appreciated in the United States, but it was created and sustained by Mexicans in Mexico. But in the late 1960s, things began to change, to the point that many musicians and supporters started to feel that it was changing too much, that if it were to change too radically, it would be diluted to the point that it would lose the very essence that made it special. In Cano's words, it would become a taco with ketchup, not with salsa.

THE THREADS OF CHANGE

As you have already learned, in the United States, many forces have been at work to change mariachi music. Some changes have been musical innovations. San Antonio's Mariachi Campanas de América, for example, has a version of their group with trombone and drum set that plays dance music from outside the mariachi realm. In order to engage audiences with no knowledge of mariachi music, they also tap the country fiddle strain of American music, playing the hoedown "The Orange Blossom Special," as do many other mariachis, as a novelty piece. José Hernández's Mariachi Sol de México has recorded an album with the Beach Boys and another with the Broadway show tune "New York, New York." You have read Hernández's explanation of this innovation as wanting to show that the mariachi was capable of working on par with these other forms of music. Most of the top groups—mariachis Los Camperos, Cobre, Campanas de América, Sol de México, and Vargas—have recorded or performed with symphony orchestras. A few mariachis have added a rap- or hip hop–style tune to their repertoire, for fun and to appeal to young people. Nearly all mariachis perform "El Mariachi Loco," a lighthearted, silly *cumbia*, written for mariachi in the dance rhythm originally from Colombia and the Caribbean.

Cobre's Randy Carrillo elaborates on his view of musical innovation within tradition:

> I think the general opinion of just about everyone is that Mariachi Cobre has a traditional niche, that we are a fairly traditional mariachi. However, people talk about the music evolving. I don't consider this instrumentation playing another genre of music, American music, or any other type of non-mariachi music, I don't consider that as being evolving. The way we have evolved the music is utilizing tools and techniques of musical betterment in playing, harmonies. Our arrangers, Frank [Grijalva] and Steve [Carrillo]—I think they have evolved the music by the utilization of some harmonies that they use. We haven't changed the core, the heart of a melody, or formats of certain songs. That tradition—the forms, the lyrics, all that—still are there, however, there are some very subtle harmonic devices that these two guys use that make us have a little different sound. To me that's more true to evolution than playing American music with this instrumentation. (Carrillo interview)

Social Threads.   Most of the more recent threads of change, however, have been social rather than musical. You have read about Nati Cano's efforts to raise the social status of mariachi music as well as to take the music to new heights of aesthetic creativity and technical proficiency. In separating the mariachi from its stigma of being a social *basura* 'trash', in his words, he had a lot of help. About the same time Cano was planning La Fonda, a number of educational programs, social movements, and Mexican-American community improvement organizations were emerging that would all help create the "very big movement" of mariachi music in the United States. Emerging independently, they eventually came together to reinforce one another.

Mariachi in Schools. In 1966, Belle Ortiz, a pianist and fourth grade teacher in the heavily Mexican-American San Antonio Independent School District, started a mariachi music program in a local elementary school. San Antonio had already proven itself fertile ground for the seeds of mariachi music in the successful efforts of Josephine Orta and her husband, Jesse, to incorporate mariachi-style music into the Catholic masses in local churches (Jonathan Clark, written communication, 2004). In the public schools, Ortiz added Spanish-language songs to the class repertoire and then started guitar classes in the fourth, fifth, and sixth grades. In 1970, she started the first mariachi-style ensemble at the high school, with trumpets, guitar, and piano. By 1975, her program was so successful that she was asked to start similar programs in eight schools. She recalls, "Our PTA enrollment just went sky high when the high school mariachi would play. Everybody wanted to come hear it. And, it was good public relations for the school district because when there was a convention, our kids would go and perform, and it was a novelty. But, I didn't want to consider this as a novelty act. I also wanted it to be considered as a strong musical program." With the help of her husband-to-be, Juan Ortiz, who had already studied both opera singing and *guitarrón*, they expanded the mariachi-in-the-schools program to nine high schools and seventeen middle schools and taught mariachi music ensembles with the traditional mariachi instrumentation and sound. The San Antonio model eventually was imitated by many schools throughout Texas.

Belle and Juan Ortiz were motivated by social and educational concerns as much as by musical ones. Says Juan,

> The thing back then [was] that if you were *mexicano*, you had to go to vocational school, because you could be a good mechanic, you could be a good upholstery guy . . . but you don't think about going to Harvard, don't think about going to all these other places. So, when we did our program, Belle made it a point that curriculum was first

. . . Belle went ahead and said, "You must maintain a C or better average, and if you didn't then you wouldn't be able to be in the performing group." . . . This is why the San Antonio district was successful, the mariachi program. That's why I think it reached as far as it did, was because of the groundwork that Belle laid in the very beginning.

Belle herself, as a Mexican high school student, had been urged to follow a secretarial career rather than go to college, but she insisted on studying to be a teacher. Later, she "went back over there and sat there

FIGURE 5.1 *Juan and Belle Ortiz pioneered both mariachi education programs in Texas and the mariachi festival movement, launching the San Antonio International Mariachi Conference in 1979.* *(Photograph by author, 2004)*

and smiled at those people, you know. . . . Same school, I went back to start the mariachi program."

At the time Belle Ortiz was beginning her elementary school program, graduate student Donn Borcherdt had started a mariachi performance class in 1961 or 1962 at UCLA in the Institute for Ethnomusicology. Elder mariachi violinist Jesús Sánchez, a native of Zacoalco, Jalisco, was found working in the fields north of Los Angeles and was hired to teach the course. Sánchez had played mariachi music in Mexico City before moving to the United States. By 1970, the student group had named itself Mariachi Uclatlán ("land of UCLA," in the Aztec Náhuatl language) and was performing professionally throughout Los Angeles. I was a member of that group. Little did Nati Cano know it at the time, but we idolized Los Camperos and would often visit La Fonda and talk about it for days afterward. By the mid-1970s, Mariachi Uclatlán had become one of the most prominent mariachis in Southern California. The fact that the University of California supported mariachi music made an important social statement about the music's value. Several of the members of that group, Mark Fogelquist, James Koetting, David Kilpatrick, and I, went on to teach, write about, and support the music in the years that followed, creating more threads of change.

School mariachi programs multiplied. In Tucson, Arizona, in 1964, a Catholic priest named Father Rourke started a student group named Los Changuitos Feos 'The Ugly Little Monkeys'. As the Changuitos matured, several members, including Randy Carrillo, his brother Steve, Gilberto Vélez, and others, formed a professional group in 1971 and called it Mariachi Cobre, in honor of Arizona being the Copper (Cobre) state. Mariachi Cobre rose to become one of the most accomplished mariachis in the United States. In 1982, they accepted an offer to perform regularly at Epcot Center in Orlando, Florida, where they have remained for more than twenty-three years. Their success and high visibility fueled the school mariachi program throughout Arizona and beyond. Randy Carrillo expresses concern that the socially fashionable desire to play mariachi music should not cause young people to ignore learning musical fundamentals.

> Don't get elementary school kids or middle school kids without any musical training, start trying to teach them mariachi music and singing, especially with some poor educator that got put in that position, who may not know that style of the music or even have access to any of it. I've seen kids ruin their voices, because they're going to go out there and sing their hearts out because this is the concept of how mariachis

sing. They dress in their *trajes*, people praise them for doing it. Sometimes they even get paid money for doing it. Well guess what? They
like that. You know? I mean, what's not to like? But they have been
done a disservice by allowing that to happen. (Carrillo interview)

Today, there are hundreds of student mariachi programs in the
United States, spread mainly throughout the Southwest, but also found
in Chicago, New York City, Washington state, and many other places.

Mark Fogelquist, formerly the director of Mariachi Uclatlán, began
the mariachi program in Wenatchee, Washington, now heads a mariachi program in Chula Vista, California, and is one of the nation's leading mariachi educators. He points to the social and educational value
of his former program in Wenatchee, especially to the children of Mexican immigrants who came to work in the apple orchards.

The Mexican kids who came into the town . . . were about five years
behind academically for their age. . . . They were in seventh grade, they
were reading at a second grade level, in Spanish. . . . Every year, thirteen or fourteen teenagers did not know the alphabet. They knew some
of the letters. None of them knew their times tables. You know, I mean,
kids who are in seventh grade, they don't know 4 times 3. So, what
they did was, almost all of them dropped out. They would go through
middle school, and once they would get into high school in the ninth
grade, they would drop out. It was like a 90 percent dropout rate. . . .
For many of these kids, the only thing they came to school for was
the mariachi. Every hour they spent, they were sitting in the back of
the room, looking stupid, and feeling stupid—feeling like failures.
They not only didn't know English, but even if they learned play-
ground English, even if they learned, you know, to get along with the
kids out on the play yard, they didn't have the academic skills to survive through the ninth grade, so they would just drop out. Well, the
mariachi, what happened in there is, they learned—they learned how
to learn, which is the most important thing of all. "Okay, we need to
master this, this concept, or this musical idea, or this song, or this
chord change, or this rhythmic pattern, and learn how to take it apart,
do it slowly, simply, over and over, and then use it as a building block
to step onto the next thing." And this carried over in the academic
world. So, I don't know what the statistics are, but the kids that got
involved in the mariachi program and that stayed with it for at least
two years . . . it transformed them. . . . Almost all of those kids have
graduated from high school. (Fogelquist interview)

FIGURE 5.2   *Mark Fogelquist teaches his mariachi class at Chula Vista High School in Chula Vista, California.*   (Photograph by author, 2004)

Fogelquist's testimony makes it easy to understand the motivation on the part of educators to support mariachi programs in the schools.

Mariachi Festivals.   Hand in hand with the growth of school programs came the mariachi festival movement. The first mariachi festival, the San Antonio International Mariachi Conference, was launched in 1979, led by Belle and Juan Ortiz. Their idea met with great resistance from some educators and politicians, resistance that reflected the hierarchical ideas of music at the time. Juan recalls them thinking:

> The best way to do it [and get the support of the establishment] is to conduct a seminar, a conference. Let's do something, and let's bring in [Mariachi] Vargas. . . . That's when the [Board of Education and the] City Council [joined in]. . . . All hell broke loose, because, well, they started accusing Belle that, first of all, "Where's it going to stop, Belle? You're trying to legitimize mariachi music, you're trying to make it a curriculum, you're trying to get a class in the classroom.

When's it going to stop? Are we going to stop at Country and Western music? Is it going to stop at R&B music?"

I worked at the National Endowment for the Arts at the time, and I let Belle and Juan Ortiz know of possible grant support for the festival. They were awarded a grant. Belle remembers, "The National Endowment for the Arts was already a heavy name that was backing up the idea, so that made it just a little bit more palatable for City Council, and fortunately, Henry Cisneros at that time was our mayor, so he had a good following behind him." The festival was inaugurated in 1979 and became an annual event. It included concerts, teaching workshops by members of the renowned Mariachi Vargas and lectures by credentialed music scholars such as Mark Fogelquist and myself, and performances by student groups. This combination of ingredients set a standard against which many other mariachi festivals that followed would be measured.

The San Antonio International Mariachi Conference model inspired other festivals, some of which included a teaching workshop component, and others that were concert performances only. In 1983, the Tucson International Mariachi Festival and Fresno's ¡Viva el Mariachi! Festival sprung up. Members of Mariachi Cobre had attended the San Antonio event, and they returned home determined to see their own festival in Tucson. The Tucson festival thrived, attracting hundreds of students and thousands of concertgoers each year over the following two decades.

Hugo Morales, the director of the nonprofit Radio Bilingüe in Fresno, had read about funding for a mariachi festival in the National Endowment for the Arts annual report and thought it was a perfect fit for the organization's community-building, educational mission. Festivals in San Jose, Los Angeles, Albuquerque, Las Cruces, El Paso, Salinas (CA), Wenatchee, and many other places followed. Radio Bilingüe was founded by farmworkers and artists in the 1970s to empower Latinos, particularly farmworkers, to use their radios to help themselves. The ¡Viva el Mariachi! Festival was a logical extension of that mission. Says Morales, "[We] see education and the education of our children and the pride in themselves as being critical to them [being] able to think positively about themselves, and to be creative and to project their energies and their intelligence through their work and contribution to others and to their families and to themselves. So that has been at the core of this."

Kathy Flores, a Mexican-American parent of a young student of mariachi music at the festival and a medical doctor, put into her own words the perspective of mariachi music being a positive social experience, a way to strengthen the family, the community, and individual self-confidence.: "Many of our kids grow up in families which are very *mex-icano*, very traditional, and they grow up with the music, and they don't have an opportunity to express what they've grown up with, what they've heard since they were born, and mariachi music programs . . . give them the opportunity to begin to express what they've heard. . . . [It] validates that it is acceptable to enjoy this kind of music."

It is interesting to note how different this perspective is from that of the class discrimination confronted by Nati Cano as a youth. In the United States, at least among a socially committed group of Mexican Americans, mariachi's social standing had been turned upside down.

SOCIAL MOVEMENTS

Chicano *Movimiento.* The Chicano *movimiento*, spurred by the civil rights movement and other social factors, coincided with the emergence of La Fonda, the UCLA mariachi program, and mariachi-in-schools programs. Many in the *movimiento* saw mariachi music as a proud symbol

FIGURE 5.3 *Students and featured mariachis perform together at the grand finale of the ¡Viva el Mariachi! Festival. (Photograph by author, 2004)*

of Mexican identity. This was a seminal time for the creation of such symbols, and the recognition of mariachi music among that generation would have an impact felt years later. *Movimiento* activist Hugo Morales explains:

> A lot of us that were in school in the sixties and seventies are now administrators and school principals, superintendants, heads of social agencies, policy makers at mid-level, and some cases, high level. So it's bound to have an impact. I mean, tomorrow, for example, at the [¡Viva el Mariachi!] Festival, you're going to have the [California] lieutenant governor, Cruz Bustamante, there. He always comes with his family, and you know, his wife and his parents. . . . And so, it's bound to have some impact.

Women's Liberation Movement. The women's liberation movement was in full swing when Mark Fogelquist was teaching a mariachi class at San José City College. One of his students there was Rebecca Gonzales, whom you read about as the first woman to pave the way for other women in the top United States mariachis. When he invited her to join Mariachi Uclatlán, he remembers that gender was not an issue.

> I wasn't really thinking about gender because . . . my experience in the mariachi world started off at UCLA. Rebecca's first exposure to mariachi music was in the class that I was teaching at San José City College, and there were a lot of girls involved in that class. And when I brought her to Mariachi Uclatlán, I was just looking for a good violinist . . . who could sing, and she was a good violinist who could sing. And, I didn't have . . . the prejudices that say, a Mexican mariachi musician who grew up in this all-male tradition would have had. I didn't carry those concepts with me. Rebecca was a fantastic person for breaking that gender barrier because she was so good. . . . It was like Jackie Robinson . . . in baseball. Who could say he didn't belong there? . . . Who could say he was thrown in just as a gimmick or something? He was good . . . , and so was Rebecca.

The fact that Rebecca Gonzales's entry into the mariachi profession coincided with the women's liberation movement helped maximize her impact on mariachi music. Nati Cano remembers both the resistance and the forces of change that surrounded her entry into his group.

> Oh, people got mad at me. "But why? Why a woman?" . . . And it was during the women's liberation movement and all that, right? The television stations came, all the major television stations. "Now at La

Fonda, a surprise . . ." And look what has occurred. That is, all of a sudden, the girls in the schools said, "Hey, it is possible. Why not?" Los Camperos . . . in the last twenty or thirty years have been an exemplar of discipline and professionalism, and La Fonda was respected worldwide for the best possible quality in mariachi music.

Pioneering women *mariacheras* such as Rebecca Gonzales, Laura Sobrino, and Rebecca's successor in Los Camperos, Mónica Treviño of Tucson, led the way for the creation of all-female mariachi groups. While a few small all-female mariachis had previously existed in Mexico and the United States, none had captured wide public attention until José Hernández recruited some of the newly developed female mariachi talent to create Mariachi Reyna de Los Ángeles in 1994. They instantly became popular and have performed at most of the principal mariachi festivals. They were followed by Mariachi Mujer Dos Mil, Las Adelitas, Las Alondras, and others. The social conventions that worked against women being included among the ranks of mariachi musicians changed significantly, expanding even more the breadth of participation in performing the music.

CONCLUSION: THE CHALLENGE OF CHANGE, THE FUTURE

The years since La Fonda opened in 1968 have seen many social innovations around mariachi music—dinner theaters, hundreds of school programs, dozens of festivals, and various community efforts to use mariachi music for social good. Interest in mariachi music has grown exponentially. Greater immigration from Mexico increased the size of the audience and the number of professional mariachi musicians in the United States. Hundreds of school and festival programs brought tens of thousands of young people to the study of mariachi music. The annual mariachi festival attendance in the United States undoubtedly exceeds 100,000. Given the extent of these changes, it might be reasonable to expect that significant changes in the music itself have followed. So what are they? Are they good or bad? Are they salsa on the taco—or ketchup?

Nati Cano offers his point of view:

> Let's see if this rings the bell. Have you seen the ad promotion . . . that says "Teach the Teachers"? . . . That's it. Depending on the quality of the teachers, that is how the young people will learn. . . . We

must not ignore the people who can contribute to the survival of the mariachi. There are many of them. . . . For example, if you go to the university . . . and you learn everything, computers—all the modern technology and all—but then you go to live in the jungle, then have them send you an Indian to tell you how you will be able to live in the jungle. So, what is happening now with the mariachi is that we are moving so fast, so fast, and we are going up each step, we are not aware of what we are doing. We are buying and selling, you understand? Surviving commercially day by day. And suddenly we are going to say, "What am I playing? This isn't mariachi anymore." Because we put ourselves so much in the commercial vein that, no more—we want to play mariachi, but it's no more . . . .

I was in a city, I think it was El Paso, right? There was a conference or a talk with the students, and I emphasized they had to learn the music of the mariachi. If they are mariachis, they have to learn the music of the mariachi. And one student asks me, "Maestro, maestro," he says, "Can I play 'Mariachi Loco' [a modern *cumbia* adapted to the mariachi]? And I told him, "yes, but I also want you to play 'Los Arrieros' or [another] *son jalisciense*." That's my theory. Change is inevitable. It is necessary. But not in exchange for the total destruction of other cultural ways.

ACTIVITY 5.1

CD track 26, entitled "Jarocho II," features Nati Cano's Mariachi Los Camperos playing their own modern arrangement of three songs borrowed from the musical tradition known as son jarocho, *native to the southern region of the state of Veracruz. While early mariachis may have used the harp, the instrument's popularity in the son jarocho tradition is reflected in its prominence in this recording. Compare the sound of the mariachi with that of some of the earliest mariachi recordings, CD tracks 4 and 6. How has Nati Cano's group preserved the earlier sounds of the mariachi, and how has the sound changed? Include the instruments, size of the group (eleven members), and style of singing in your comparisons.*

José Hernández also expressed concerns about how the popularity of the festivals leads to the loss of important mariachi repertoire and skills:

"It's really getting dangerous now with the festivals, because they give the impression of something that is not. There are mariachis that just get together just for festivals. They don't even know more than twenty songs. They just get together to go do the gig and they buy suits together. [If you tell them] 'Listen, play such-and-such a song in such-and-such a key for this singer,' they don't know it unless they study it during the week—they can't accompany you in another key." He offers this piece of advice for the teachers: "Be careful. Don't do it just to do it—'Well, you know, I'm going to make a little extra money teaching here.' But really try to search for the power—no, the passion and the spirit of the music—because the music *is* contagious. And when . . . they develop a great liking for Mexican music, the same respect will come to their teaching the music."

Pepe Martínez also offered a critique of the festival movement in the United States:

> What is happening is very strong. . . . The conferences that they are doing all over the place has been a step forward. What's happening is that there is a mistake on the part of the parents there. They think that by going to a conference for three or four days, [the kids] are going to play professionally. And if you are going to [learn] three songs, well, how can you be a professional? That is acquired [by playing] *al talón*. . . . You have to immerse yourself in it. . . . You have to play at home. . . . You have to study elsewhere, and you will learn other songs and be in a group.

Margarito Gutiérrez, a veteran mariachi who works both in Guadalajara and Los Angeles, sees the mariachi tradition more from the point of view of a career professional musician. As to the future of the mariachi, he sees it as "very good . . . in the sense that it is a very good profession. . . . It can compare well, the mariachi profession, with many other professions that are without work. Here [in Mexico] there are many college graduates, you know, who just finish their college training and there is no place for them, and they work as a bricklayer and . . . other things."

There was universal agreement among all the musicians I interviewed that the technical competence of young professional mariachis is greater than ever, that the popularity of the music and the professional opportunity for the musicians is on the increase, and that the past half-century has produced many innovations and technical challenges that have been assets to the music. Their mutual concern lies more in the future connection of mariachi music to itself—to its essential stylis-

FIGURE 5.4   *A mariachi mural adorns a business building near the Plaza de los Mariachis in East Los Angeles.*   *(Photograph by author, 1999)*

tic ingredients—and to the depth of its beauty and meaning to the people who appreciate it. Their differences lie more in their opinions of exactly what are the limits that define these ingredients, in Nati Cano's words, differentiating between "the things that are classic" and "the things that are not of importance."

Defining these limits, of course, is a matter of subjective, personal opinion, and there will never be complete agreement. Cano himself said that "it is not good for humanity for everyone to be the same." What Cano, Hernández, Martínez, and other mariachi leaders are calling for is that musicians and audiences alike immerse ourselves in the full breadth and depth of mariachi culture so that we can create a future for the mariachi that fills it with musical beauty and deep meaning for those of us who appreciate it. Do we want tacos with salsa, or tacos with ketchup? It's for all of us to decide. The more we know as musicians and consumers and the more we apply our knowledge to support the best of the music, the more we will contribute to the well-being of future mariachi culture. This, of course, is the purpose of this book.

Glossary

Adorno "Ornament" being its literal meaning, in mariachi culture, it also refers to the metal ornaments on the *traje de charro* and to the ornamental countermelodies played by the trumpets and/or violins during songs.

Al talón Its literal translation being "on the heel of the shoe," *al talón* refers to the performance context in which the mariachi moves from client to client, table to table, and establishment to establishment, seeking customers and charging by the song played.

Apodo Nickname. *Apodos,* nicknames given to most mariachi musicians, are a form of insider knowledge and humor, a dimension of the social "glue" that holds mariachi musicians together as a community. Examples are Santa Claus, El Capiro (The Capiro Tree), El Camarón (The Shrimp), La Perra (The Bitch), El Pájaro (The Bird), La Campeona (The Championess), El Pescado (The Fish), El Huichol (The Huichol Indian), El Esponjado (The Spongey One), El Gorila (The Gorilla).

Armonía (pl. armonías) In general, *armonía* means "harmony." In the mariachi, however, it takes on the special meaning of the instrumental section comprised of the *guitarrón*, six-stringed guitar, and *vihuela*. This *armonía* section, sometimes referred to in the plural—"*las armonías*"—provides the chordal-rhythmic framework for the music the mariachi plays. The *guitarrón* player provides a bass line, and the *vihuela* and guitar players strum a rhythmic-chordal pattern in unison. This use of the term *armonía* might best be translated into American English as "rhythm section."

Arpa Harp. The harp occasionally present in the modern mariachi, stands about five feet tall and has thirty-two to thirty-six nylon strings attached at one end to a soundbox with three sound holes on the side facing forward. Unlike its orchestral cousin, the concert harp, it is played in a standing position. Historically, the *arpa* might have played a major melodic and bass line role in the smaller, rural mariachi ensembles. Today, however, it may simply double the bass line played by the *guitarrón* and occasionally be foregrounded in the musical texture.

Bolero, bolero ranchero   The origins of the Mexican *bolero*, a slow-tempo, duple-meter category of music suitable for dancing, are thought to be in 1880s Cuba, where it first emerged. As the Cuban *bolero* spread abroad, it was imitated in parts of Mexico. The first distinctly Mexican popular *bolero* is thought to be "Morenita Mía," composed by Armando Villarreal in 1921. The *bolero*'s popularity endured, and in the late 1940s, suave-sounding, romance-enhancing guitar trios such as Trío Los Panchos squared off the syncopated Cuban rhythmic underpinnings to create the modern Mexican *bolero* feel of 1-(rest)-3-4. As the mariachi adapted the *bolero* to its own instrumentation, marked by the 1949 recording of "Amorcito Corazón," the *bolero ranchero* 'country-style *bolero*' emerged.

Canción ranchera (also, ranchera; pl. canciones rancheras)   *Canción* 'song', followed by the adjective *ranchera* 'country,' 'from the ranch', describes the Mexican song tradition that rose to international popularity along with, but not exclusively tied to, the mariachi. It played a prominent role in the *comedia ranchera* 'country comedy', a category of Mexican film spurred by the prototype *Allá en el Rancho Grande* (1936), favored by audiences for decades throughout Latin America. The *canción ranchera* most often is a simple, two-part song delivered by a soloist (male or female) in an extroverted, emotional style.

Chamba   "Gig," in American English. A musical engagement for a special occasion in which the mariachi is paid by the hour or time playing.

Charro   Mexican cowboy. The mariachi musician's image as a *charro* 'country gentleman' went hand-in-hand with its close association with idealized images of Mexican ranch life during the emergence of the ultra-popular *comedia ranchera* 'country comedy' films beginning with *Allá en el Rancho Grande* (1936). Even though mariachi musicians are often called *charros*, and while there is great similarity between mariachi uniforms and the traditional show dress of Mexican cowboys, there nevertheless are important differences as well, and the two groups keep separate identities. While horse-mounted *charros* may wear showy but practical garb at ceremonial events and *jaripeos* 'competitive rodeos', mariachi dress is tailored more for show and less for riding horses, which many mariachi *charros* have never attempted.

Copla Poetic stanza employed in many regional styles of Mexican *mestizo* music. A *copla* is commonly comprised of four to six octosyllabic lines with even-numbered lines rhyming. Often some or all of the lines in the *copla* may be repeated, stretching the length of the sung section and improving the listeners' chances of understanding the text.

Corrido Narrative ballad. Most likely deriving from the Spanish *romance,* in which *copla* after *copla* is sung to a repeated strophic melody to tell an often epic story, the *corrido* in Mexico is historically associated with its apogee during the Mexican Revolution (1910–17). Often referred to as a musical "newspaper," *corridos* recount real or imagined events, memorializing and/or idealizing them in the process. The *corrido's* popularity continues today, particularly in the repertoire of the accordion-driven *conjunto norteño* 'northern-style combo', associated with Mexico's northern border region.

Diana A short flourish, usually the last section of the "Jarabe Tapatío" (known to some as the "Mexican Hat Dance"), played by the mariachi to mark special moments, such as toasts or other ceremonial points calling for applause.

Grito Yell. *Gritos* mark emotion-packed moments in mariachi music, especially during *sones* and *canciones rancheras*. Listeners or musicians may spontaneously let out a *grito* when moved by the music or (by the musician) for dramatic effect. While *gritos* may be spontaneous and varied in sound, they nevertheless tend to fall within certain culturally determined stylistic parameters.

Guitarrón (pl. *guitarrones*) The *guitarrón* is the bass instrument of the mariachi. Its eight-shaped, soundbox with a spined, convex back is much larger than that of the guitar or *vihuela*. Its size and the lightweight, sonorous tropical cedar wood of which it is made create a full, voluminous, low-pitched dimension to the mariachi sound. Its six strings are tuned A^1-D-G-c-e-A. The *guitarronero* '*guitarrón* player' plays most notes by plucking two strings at a time, producing either a unison or an octave. Together with the *vihuela* and six-stringed guitar, it forms the mariachi instrumental section called *armonía* 'rhythm section'.

Huapango *Huapango* (pronounced wah-PAHNG-oh) is thought to derive from the Náhuatl Indian phrase *cuauh-panco* 'on top of the wood', referring to a dance tradition of northeastern Mexico's Huasteca region. The dance traditionally was performed on a wooden platform and was accompanied by a regional style of music, with violin and two regional guitars strummed in a distinctive rhythmic fashion. The singing was often ornamented with falsetto breaks. Mariachi musicians and songwriters evolved a *huapango* style of their own, drawing from the Huastecan *huapango*'s rhythms or singing style.

Jarabe *Jarabe* most likely derives from its meaning as syrup ("sweet," by extension), but in the mariachi context, it usually refers to a multisectioned folk dance. First documented in writing in the late 1700s, the *jarabe* is historically associated with the emergence of Mexican *mestizo* culture. Over time, many *jarabes* took the form of a "dance medley," a string of distinctive melodic segments, each with its own accompanying dance step. The most famous *jarabe* is "Jarabe Tapatío," known to some as the "Mexican Hat Dance" or the "Jarabe Nacional / National Jarabe."

Joropo This fast-tempo, triple-meter musical genre hails from the plains ranching culture of the Orinoco river basin, overlapping Venezuela and Colombia in northern South America. In its contemporary traditional form, the *joropo* is played by a folk harp, maracas, bass, and *cuatro* 'small four-stringed guitar'. Its popularity has surpassed its historical geographical boundaries, and its syncopated guitar rhythm has been adopted by musicians of other nations and cultures, including mariachis.

Mariachada Slang term, meaning the mariachi community.

Mariache This archaic form of mariachi reflects a frequent form of its pronunciation, particularly among rural communities. The similarity of *mariache* to the written version of the French word *mariage* 'wedding' may in part account for the often cited but completely erroneous, etymology of the word *mariachi* as deriving from the French word.

Mariachero/a   Slang term, mariachi musician.

Mariachi (also, *mariachi moderno*)   In modern times, mariachi refers to an individual mariachi musician, to a mariachi ensemble, or, as an adjective, to something identified with either of these, such as "mariachi repertoire." The mariachi musician is archetypically featured with tightly tailored pants and jacket with metal or embroidered ornaments. The mariachi ensemble's instrumentation typically includes two to five violins, one or two trumpets, *guitarrón, vihuela,* and six-stringed guitar. A large harp might be included in a large-scale mariachi, sometimes known as a *mariachi de lujo* 'deluxe mariachi', or in archaic-style groups. In the nineteenth century, "mariachi" might have described a festive event in western Mexico that featured secular musicians and might have included drinking, dancing, and gambling. It might also have designated a drum, a dance platform, or a group of musicians in that region. *Mariachi moderno* refers to the modern mariachi instrumentation that crystallized in the early 1950s. While the origin of the term *mariachi* is uncertain, its often-mentioned etymological link to the French word *mariage* has been proven to be false by its presence in documents that precede the French occupation of Mexico in the 1860s.

Mariachi culture   Mariachi culture embraces the social, cultural, and economic contexts of the music and the musicians. Understanding how the forces of these contexts come to bear on music performance itself helps us understand more deeply the meaning and dynamics of the music.

Mestizo   The results of the mixing of races and cultures in Latin American colonial times. In Mexico, the *mestizaje* (mixing) of European, Indian, and African peoples led to *mestizos,* accounting for over three-quarters of the country's population of over 100 million.

Planta   A *planta* is a regular engagement, for example, a restaurant performance every Friday from 7 p.m. to 10 p.m. Typically, the establishment pays the mariachi group a negotiated regular fee, augmented by tips from the clientele.

Polka (also, *polca*)   The late-nineteenth-century European vogue of the polka as a preferred social dance reached Mexico, as many Mexicans still looked to Europe for their cultural models. From the close of the nineteenth century into the first decades of the twentieth century, many Mexican composers wrote original polkas, many of which proved to be enduring, such as "Jesusita en Chihuahua."

Quinceañera (also, *quince años*) In the United States, *quinceañera* refers both to the celebration of a fifteen-year-old woman's passage to maturity and to the person being celebrated. In Mexico, the event may more often be called a *quince años* celebration. People often mark the occasion with mariachi music.

Seguidilla In the *seguidilla* poetic stanza form, lines alternative between seven and five syllables, with *abcb* being the typical rhyme pattern of a four-line stanza. A "filler" phrase such as "cielito lindo" may be interjected between the seven- and five-syllable lines in order to fill out the melodic phrasing.

Serenata For the mariachi, the *serenata* is a popular type of *chamba* that accommodates clients desiring a short serenade to mark a special occasion, rather than an hour or more of music. *Serenatas* may be consist of seven or eight pieces and be about a half-hour in duration.

Son (pl. *sones*) In Mexico, *son* may refer to a regional style of *mestizo* music or to certain melodies of Indian cultural groups. In both cases, most *sones* have a rhythmic drive appropriate for dancing. Regional *mestizo son* traditions may be distinguished by instrumentation, instrumental technique, singing style, repertoire, and other traits. These *sones* most often are structured around *versos* (sung poetic stanzas) alternating with instrumental interludes. In contrast, Indian *sones* tend to consist of one or two short melodic phrases, performed instrumentally and repeated at length. *Son* also may be used generally to mean simply "tune" or "sound," reflecting its principal usage in pre-nineteenth-century Mexican colonial times.

Son jarocho The *son jarocho* is a regional style of *son*, rooted in the southern coastal plain of the eastern Mexican state of Veracruz. In the professional realm of folk-derived popular music, the *son jarocho* is often associated with the harp and with pieces such as "La Bamba," "El Cascabel," and "El Balajú."

Tapatío/a An adjective or noun describing a person or thing associated with the city of Guadalajara and the surrounds, a city closely linked to mariachi music and image.

Traje de charro **(also, *traje*)** Through the portrayal of the mariachi through movies and public presentations as a *charro* 'country gentleman', the *traje de charro* became the iconic dress of the modern professional mariachi's "country gentleman" image. The mariachi *traje de charro* is designed for show, while the *charro* horseman's *traje* is designed to meet the requirements of horsemanship.

Vihuela The *vihuela*, along with the *guitarrón* and six-stringed guitar, supplies the rhythmic and chordal framework for the music played by the mariachi. It has an eight-shaped soundbox with a spined, convex back and five strings tuned A-d-g-B-e. *Vihuela* chord fingerings are similar to those of the six-stringed guitar, though without the guitar's low-pitched E string. The *vihuelero* '*vihuela* player' employs defined hand patterns of strumming called *mánicos* to create a rhythmic background. Together with the *guitarrón* and the six-stringed guitar, it forms the mariachi instrumental section called *armonía* 'rhythm section'.

References

Aguilar, Ignacio. Apuntes biográficos del Sr. Canónigo Don. . . . Zamora, Mexico: Tipografía de la Escuela de Artes y Oficius, n.d.

Barrios de los Ríos, Enrique. Paisajes de occidente. Sombrerete, Zacatecas, Mexico: Biblioteca Estarsiana, 1908.

Clark, Jonathan. Introduction to liner notes to Mexico's Pioneer Mariachis, Vol. 4. Cuarteto Coculense: The Very First Mariachi Recordings, 1908–1909. Arhoolie Folklyric CD 7036.

———. Liner notes to Mexico's Pioneer Mariachis, Vol. 1. Mariachi Coculense "Rodríguez" de Cirilo Marmolejo, 1926–1936. Arhoolie Folklyric CD 7011. www.arhoolie.com.

———. Liner notes to Mexico's Pioneer Mariachis, Vol. 2. Mariachi Tapatío de José Marmolejo. Arhoolie Folklyric CD 7012. www.arhoolie.com.

Jáuregui, Jesús. El Mariachi: Símbolo Musical de México. Mexico, D.F.: Banpaís, 1990.

Pearlman, Steven Ray. "Standardization and Innovation in Mariachi Music Performance in Los Angeles." Pacific Review of Ethnomusicology 1:1–12, 1984.

Rafael, Hermes. Los Primeros Mariachis en la Ciudad de México: Guía para el Investigador. Mexico, D.F.: privately published by author, 1999.

Ramo de Inquisición, tomos 1052, 1297. Archivos de la Nación documents of Spanish Inquisition in Mexico, 1766.

Sheehy, Daniel. Liner notes to Mariachi Los Camperos de Nati Cano, ¡Viva el Mariachi! Nati Cano's Mariachi Los Camperos. Smithsonian Folkways Recordings SF 40459. www.folkways.si.edu.

Sonnichsen, Philip, and Jonathan Clark, with assistance from Hermes Rafael and Jim Nicolopulos. Liner notes to Mexico's Pioneer Mariachis, Vol. 1. Mariachi Coculense "Rodríguez" de Cirilo Marmolejo, 1926–1936. Arhoolie Folklyric CD 7011. www.arhoolie.com.

CD Liner Notes

Mariachi Los Camperos de Nati Cano. *¡Viva el Mariachi! Nati Cano's Mariachi Los Camperos.* Smithsonian Folkways Recordings SF 40459. Liner notes by Daniel Sheehy. www.folkways. si.edu.

Mariachi Mujer Das Mil. *La Nueva Imagen del Milenio.* Self-published recording. www. mariachimujer2000.com.

Mariachi Sol de México de José Hernández. *Sentimiento Ranchero.* Serenata Records. www. mariachi-sol.com.

Mexico's Pioneer Mariachis, Vol. 1. Mariachi Coculense "Rodríguez" de Cirilo Marmolejo, 1926–1936. Arhoolie Folklyric CD 7011. Liner notes by Philip Sonnichsen and Jonathan Clark, with assistance from Hermes Rafael and Jim Nicolopulus. www. arhoolie.com.

Mexico's Pioneer Mariachis, Vol. 2. Mariachi Tapatío de José Marmolejo. Arhoolie Folklyric CD 7012. Liner notes by Jonathan Clark. www.arhoolie.com.

 *Mexico's Pioneer Mariachis, Vol. 4. Cuarteto Coculense: The Very First Mariachi Recordings, 1908–1909.* Arhoolie Folklyric CD 7036. Liner notes by Jonathan Clark and Hermes Rafael. www. arhoolie.com.

Interviews

Cano, Natividad. Interview with author. Fillmore, CA, August 7, 1999.

Carrillo, Randy, Steve Carrillo, Héctor Gama, and Francisco Grijalva. Interview with author. Orlando, FL, February 20, 2002.

Clark, Jonathan. Written exchange, 2004.

Flores, Kathy. Interview with author. Fresno, CA, March 24, 2000.

Fogelquist, Mark. Interview with author. Fresno, CA, March 25, 2000.

Gonzales, Rebecca. Interview with author. Palos Verdes, CA, March 23, 2000.

Gutiérrez, Margarito. Interview with author. Guadalajara, Jalisco, Mexico, March 2, 1997.

Hernández, José. Interview with author. Wenatchee, WA, April 19, 2000.

Martínez Barajas, José "Pepe." Interview with author. Guadalajara, Jalisco, Mexico, August 31, 2001.

Moreno, Carmencristina. Interview with author. Fresno, California, July 11, 2002.

Morales, Hugo. Interview with author. Fresno, CA, March 25, 2000.

Ortiz, Juan, and Belle Ortiz. Interview with author. San Antonio, TX, June 16, 2000.

Pérez, Leonor Xóchitl. Interview with author. Los Angeles, CA, April 11, 2000.

Sobrino, Laura. Interview with author. Whittier, CA, April 12, 2000.

Resources

Written Resources

Chamorro Escalante, J. Arturo. *Mariachi Antiguo, Jarabe y Son: Símbolos Compartidos y Tradición Musical en las Identidades Jaliscienses*. Zapopan, Jalisco, Mexico: Colegio de Jalisco, 2000.

Fogelquist, Mark. "Mariachi Conferences and Festivals in the United States." In ed. Elizabeth Peterson, *The Changing Faces of Tradition: A Report on the Folk and Traditional Arts in the United States*, 18–23. Research division report 38. Washington, D.C.: National Endowment for the Arts, 1996.

———. "Rhythm and Form in the Contemporary *Son Jalisciense*." Master's thesis, University of California at Los Angeles, 1975.

Fogelquist, Mark, and Patricia W. Harpole. *Los Mariachis! An Introduction to Mexican Mariachi Music*. Danbury, CT: World Music Press, 1989.

Galindo, Blas. "El Mariachi." *Boletín del Departamento de Música de la Secretaría de Educación Pública* 1:3–8, 1946.

Gradante, William. "'El Hijo del Pueblo': José Alfredo Jiménez and the Mexican Canción Ranchera." *Latin American Music Review* 3(1):36–59, 1982.

Jáquez, Cándida F. "Meeting la Cantante through Verse, Song, and Performance." In *Chicana Traditions: Continuity and Change*, ed. Norma E. Cantú and Olga Nájera-Ramírez. Urbana and Chicago: University of Illinois Press, 2002.

Jáuregui, Jesús. *Los Mariachis de Mi Tierra . . . Noticias, Cuentos, Testimonios y Conjeturas: 1925–1994*. Mexico, D.F.: Consejo Nacional para la Cultura y las Artes, Dirección General de Culturas Populares, 1999.

Pérez, Leonor Xóchitl. "Transgressing the Taboo: A Chicana's Voice in the Mariachi World." In *Chicana Traditions: Continuity and Change*, ed. Norma E. Cantú and Olga Nájera-Ramírez. Urbana and Chicago: University of Illinois Press, 2002.

Rafael, Hermes. *Origen e Historia del Mariachi*. Mexico: Editorial Katún. S.A., 1983.

Reuter, Jas. *La Música Popular de México: Origen e Historia de la Música Que Canta y Toca el Pueblo Mexicano*. Mexico, D.F.: Panorama Editorial, 1985.

Saldívar, Gabriel. *El Jarabe, Baile Popular Mexicano*. Mexico, D.F.: Talleres Gráficos de la Nación, 1937.

Sheehy, Daniel. "Mexican Mariachi Music: Made in the USA." In *Musics of Multicultural America*, ed. Kip Lornell and Anne K. Rasmussen, 131–54. New York: Schirmers Books, 1997.

———. "Mexico." In *The Garland Encyclopedia of World Music, Vol. 2: South America, Mexico, Central America, and the Caribbean*. New York: Garland Publishing, 1998: 600–25.

———. "Overview of Hispanic-American Music: Mexican *Mestizo* Music and Afro-Cuban Music." In *Teaching Music with a Multicultural Approach*, ed. William M. Anderson. 70–75. Reston, VA: Music Educators National Conference, 1991.

———. "Popular Mexican Music Traditions: The Mariachi of West Mexico and the Conjunto Jarocho of Veracruz." In ed. John Schechter, *Music in Latin American Culture: Regional Traditions*, 34–79. New York: Schirmer Books, 1999.

Sounds of the World. Music of Latin America: Mexico, Ecuador, Brazil. Reston, VA: Music Educators National Conference, 1987. Three cassettes. Study guide by Dale A. Olsen, Daniel E. Sheehy, and Charles A. Perrone.

CD Liner Notes

Mariachi Los Camperos de Nati Cano. *¡Llegaron Los Camperos! Concert Favorites of Nati Cano's Mariachi Los Camperos*. Smithsonian Folkways Recordings SF 40517. www.folkways.si.edu.

Mexico's Pioneer Mariachis, Vol. 3. Mariachi Vargas de Tecalitlán: Their First Recordings, 1937–1947. Arhoolie Folklyric CD 7015. Liner notes by Jonathan Clark. www.arhoolie.com.

Compact Discs for Listening

Aceves Mejía, Miguel. *El Gallo Colorado: Miguel Aceves Mejía con el Mariachi Vargas de Tecalitlán.* BMG Entertainment México (RCA) 743215376828.

Aguilar, Antonio. *Antonio Aguilar.* Discos Musart 038.

————. *Rancheras de relajo.* Discos Musart 035.

Aguilar, Pepe. *Pepe Aguilar: Por Mujeres Como Tú.* Discos Musart 7-509985-318192.

Beltrán, Lola. *Lola Beltrán "La Grande."* Discos Peerless PCD-014-8.

Campanas de América. *Campanas de América.* Tejas 2003.

Charro Avitia. *Charro Avitia . . . El Bandolero! Con el Mariachi Vargas de Tecalitlán y el Mariachi México.* Bertelsmann de México 74321419042.

Domingo, Plácido. *100 Años de Mariachi.* EMI Latin H2-7243-5-56925-2-8.

Fernández, Vicente. *Mexicanísimo: 24 Éxitos.* Sony Discos CDA-80918.

————. *Tesoros Musicales de México. 16 Éxitos Originales.* Discos CBS International CDDI-10415.

Gabriel, Juan. *Juan Gabriel en el Palacio de Bellas Artes con la Orquesta Sinfónica Nacional.* BMG Music (RCA) 2498-2-RL.

————. *15 Años de Éxitos Rancheros.* BMG (RCA) 3208-2-RL.

Infante, Pedro. *Antología: Serenata con Pedro Infante.* WEA International 49348.

Jiménez, José Alfredo. *Lo Mejor de José Alfredo Jiménez: 33 Grandes Éxitos.* BMG (RCA) 2254-2-RL.

Los Cenzontles, with Julián González. *El Chivo. Traditional Mariachi Volume III.* Los Cenzontles Mexican Arts Center.

Mariachi Cobre. *Este Es Mi Mariachi.* Kuckuck Schallplatten 11105-2. www.harmonies.com.

————. *Mariachi Cobre.* Kuckuck Schallplatten 11095-2. www.harmonies.com.

————. *XXV Aniversario.* Black Sun Music 15022-2.

Mariachi México de Pepe Villa. 1998. *Danzones.* Discos Musart 1821.

————. *Mariachi.* Musart CDN-002.

————. *Más Mariachi!* Mediterráneo MCD-10130.

Mariachi Reyes del Aserradero. *Sones from Jalisco.* Discos Corason COCD108.

Mariachi Reyna de Los Angeles. *Serenata Records.* www.mariachi-sol.com.

Mariachi Sol de México de José Hernández. *New York, New York.* Serenata Records. www.mariachi-sol.com.

————. *La Nueva Era del Mariachi Sol de México de José Hernández.* EMI Latin H272438348642. www.mariachi-sol.com.

————. *Tequila con Limón con el Mariachi Sol de México de José Hernández.* Fonovisa FPCD-10183. www.mariachi-sol.com

Mariachi Vargas de Tecalitlán. *100 años de música.* BMG 7-4321902742-9.

————. *La Fiesta del Mariachi.* PolyGram Discos 7-31452-69462-1.

————. *El Mariachi.* PolyGram Discos 8393322.

————. *Mariachi Vargas Sinfónico*. Acompañado por la Orquesta Filarmónica del Estado de Querétaro. n.p. [private pressing] RF-102.

————. *Mariachi Vargas de Tecalitlán: Colección Mi Historia*. PolyGram Discos 731453-7852-2.

————. *El Mejor Mariachi del Mundo*. RCA International 53177. Reissue of 1958 original.

————. *Música de América*. Peerless PCD-012-1.

————. *La "Nueva" Dimensión. Versión Original de La Bikina con Mariachi Vargas de Tecalitlán*. RCA Records 74321-42057-2.

————. *Rubén Fuentes 1944–1994: 50 Años con Su Música y Arreglos para el Mejor Mariachi del Mundo*. PolyGram Discos 731452-62232.

Mejía, Miguel Aceves. *Los Grandes de la Música Ranchera*. BMG (RCA) 74321-11106-2.

————. *20 Éxitos*. BMG (RCA) CDM-3347.

Mendoza, Amalia. *La Tariacuri*. RCA International.

Negrete, Jorge. *15 Éxitos*. RCA CDM-3018.

Peña, Ezequiel. *15 Kilates Musicales*. Fonovisa SDCD-6110.

Reyes, Gerardo. *15 Zarpazos con Gerardo Reyes*. Sony Music Entertainment (CBS) (Mexico) 037628-24272-7.

Reyes, Lucha. *20 Éxitos. Serie Platino*. RCA International 60512.

Ronstadt, Linda. *Canciones de Mi Padre*. Electra/Asylum Records 970765.

Solís, Javier. *Boleros del Alma*. Sony Discos CDZ-81488.

————. *15 Auténticos Éxitos. Rancheras con Javier Solís*. Sony Discos (CBS) CDB-81027.

————. *Rancheras con Javier Solís*. CBS CDB-80353.

Villa, Lucha. *Lucha Villa con Mariachi: Colección de Oro*. Balboa 2805.

DVD Resources for Viewing

Mariachi: The Spirit of Mexico. Leo Eaton, producer/director. Produced by WLIW (New York) in association with KCET (Los Angeles).

Pasajero: A Journey of Time and Memory: A Documentary by Ricardo Braojos & Eugene Rodríguez. Los Cenzontles Mexican Arts Center. www.loscenzontles.com.

¡Viva el Mariachi! The History, the Culture, the Instruments of Mariachi Music. Al Gonzalez, Vision Quest Entertainment. www.visionquestent.com.

Index

Note: Page numbers in *italics* refer to figures or photos.